GOD'S GOOD FRUIT

Raymond Tomkinson

GOD'S GOOD FRUIT

A study course on the
FRUIT OF THE SPIRIT

RAYMOND
TOMKINSON

First published in 2002 by
KEVIN MAYHEW LTD
Buxhall, Stowmarket, Suffolk IP14 3BW
E-mail: info@kevinmayhewltd.com

9 8 7 6 5 4 3 2 1 0

ISBN 1 84003 860 8
Catalogue No. 1500480

Cover design by Angela Selfe
Edited by Katherine Laidler
Typesetting by Louise Selfe

Printed and bound in Great Britain

This book is dedicated to my dear daughter Marian:
gift of Joy; fruit of Love

Acknowledgements

Once again, I thank my beloved wife Rose and our daughter for their understanding, wisdom and encouragement throughout this project. Their observations, insights and comments have been immensely valuable.

I am deeply indebted to the Revd Professor Mark Williams, Director of the Institute of Medical and Social Care Research, University of Wales, Bangor. Without his professional advice, profound wisdom, and personal friendship I would not have been able to complete this work.

So many people have been supportive that it is hazardous to mention only a few but I would like to thank the Revd Philip Collins for his endless patience, for his prayerful support and spiritual advice. Thanks to Bishop Geoffrey Rowell and Archdeacon John Guille who have encouraged me to complete this project, and thanks to friends and colleagues at Old Alresford Place and in the parishes where I have served. Thanks to so many good friends. Last, but by no means least, I would like to thank the people whose own contemplation of virtue, shared in confidence, has contributed to this book.

RAYMOND TOMKINSON

But the fruit of the Spirit
is love, joy, peace,
patience, kindness, goodness,
faithfulness, gentleness, and self-control;
against such there is no law.

Galatians 5:22, 23

Contents

Introduction

Sophie is quite old now. She has lived through two world wars, through the depression of the 1930s and numerous economic recessions since. She lives alone but has loving and supportive friends and neighbours. Sophie no longer reads the newspapers or watches television, and she no longer listens to the news on the radio. It is not that she is either sight- or hearing-impaired, and she has what she calls 'all her facilities'. Her rejection of the media is part of her survival strategy. She finds the continual bombardment of sensational and negative 'news' too much of an attack on her dearly held view that human nature is basically good. She is not naïve. She has personal experience of some of the most destructive and wicked behaviour of which humankind is capable, but she has also known, and continues to experience, human kindness and goodness. In her relationships she has known faithfulness and patience. As well as sorrow there has been joy. In old age and infirmity she is grateful for the patience and gentleness of others. She attributes her great age to temperate self-control and admires this virtue in others.

In summary, Sophie would say she has found love in its many rich and life-giving forms. Through her experience of the very best of human nature, she has found God. By what she says and by how she lives, Sophie states, very adequately, the case for 'common grace' – the God who is at work transforming humanity so as to become like Christ. Sophie does not distinguish between those who profess a faith in Jesus Christ and those who don't. She recognises only that people reflect, to a greater or lesser degree, God-like virtues. For Sophie, there is little distinction to be made between virtues that are 'fruit' of God's grace, and the God who graces the world with his life-changing and life-enhancing presence. 'Sophie' is no one person but many who believe that humanity is not in such bad shape, even allowing for all that is tragic, lamentable, hateful, or lost.

As Sophie points to virtue in herself and in others, she points to God. She is being prophetic, and prophecy needs to be accompanied by wisdom and discernment. To point to a man leaning patiently in a dark doorway and to say, 'There is patience: there is God' would be erroneous if that man was waiting to commit a heinous crime. Likewise, lust that masquerades as love is no virtue. Kindness that is a prelude to exploitation is not kindness at all. So, when are such virtues God-like? When are they signs of the transforming activity of God at work in his world? Is it only when the virtuous are professedly Christian? Christians, like others, are not perfect; virtue and vice jostle for the best seats in the arena of human behaviour.

We may hold that Christ is found only in perfect Christians, or that in all *true* virtue Christ is glimpsed to a greater or lesser degree. *Ubi caritas et amor. Ubi caritas Deus ibi est* – Where charity and love are found, God himself is there.[*]

By exploring what St Paul calls 'The Fruit of the Spirit'[†] we may tease out the complexity and discover a simplicity that satisfies both Sophie and us. The exercise may help us to be optimistic about humanity and to offset, to some degree, the sense of hopelessness and despair felt by many – itself a destructive force that works against God's plan of transforming his people and establishing his kingdom.

Some, I know, are afraid that a broader acceptance of virtue as a sign of the presence of God may lead to complacency about conversion to Christ. However, the doctrine of salvation, through profession of Christ-centred faith, may not be in opposition to the doctrine of common grace. In the wisdom of 'Sophie' the two may not be so polarised. We may yet discover that God's strategy for the transformation of the world requires both. This book is a tiny contribution to that possibility.

As we journey through the nine-fold fruit in this book, we shall contemplate each virtue in the reverse order to the way they have come down to us in scripture. I have chosen this approach for two reasons. Firstly, because changing the order makes me stop and think about each one, just because the ordering is unfamiliar.

[*] Jacques Berthier (1923-1994), Taizé Community, France   [†] Galatians 5:22, 23

Secondly, because I wanted to draw the reader up a hillside where Love is the summit of virtue in the way that Paul describes it in his first letter to the Corinthians.* *En route*, we will challenge each virtue and allow each to challenge us. The greatest challenge may be the contemplation of God, in virtue, in the people around us. To illustrate something of my hypothesis, I would like to ponder a little on fruit (the kind in the fruit bowl), considering it as a metaphor.

Nowadays, fruit is available to us throughout the year and in enormous variety. All this is in great contrast to when I was a child growing up just after the Second World War. In those days, fresh fruit appeared on two occasions only: at Christmas, and when someone was ill. The fruit consisted of apples, pears, and bananas (which made a dramatic reappearance after the war) and, especially if someone was sick, there would be grapes. At Christmas there were oranges too, of course, and into the fruit bowl would be stuffed a packet of dates and a packet of figs. The fruit was proudly displayed on the sideboard, in a cut-glass bowl won by my grandad when playing dominoes in 1938.

The fruit was a sign. First it was a sign of caring: the sick deserved the best available. This came home to me when I was about 4 years old. My father was driving my mother and me to Dover in an old Austin 7, the luggage piled high on the roof, when the car turned over in the road. Thankfully, none of us was seriously injured. my first cry was 'Look what's happened to my bucket and spade'; my Dad's reaction, 'Never mind your bucket and spade: look at my car!'

Shocked and upset, I was sitting on the edge of the pavement when a woman came out of a nearby house and offered me a peach. I was frightened of the peach, having never before felt anything with a skin of that texture. The woman was a warm and caring person with a soothing voice. She encouraged me to eat the fruit, and so I did. I thought it the most delicious thing I had ever tasted, and I was enormously restored both by her kindness and by the fruit that symbolised it. Healed by a peach, one might

* 1 Corinthians 13

say! Thanks to her kindness we were all able to continue our journey by public transport and to enjoy our holiday by the sea.

Second, fruit at Christmas was a sign of celebration. It seemed to say that all good things come out of Christmas, especially the birth of Jesus for the salvation of the world. Fruit in the bowl on the sideboard went along with a fire in the grate, mince pies cooking in the oven, and carols on the wireless. Such things were signs of all that is good.

Where I grew up, fruit on the sideboard was also a sign of wealth. If I went to other people's homes, on the posh side of Coventry, and found fruit on the sideboard, and it wasn't Christmas and no one was ill, I knew I was in a wealthy home. Fruit is the produce of plenteousness, and, keeping to fruit as a metaphor, is a sign of a generous God who pours out a rich harvest of virtue in his people.

Jesus spoke of fruit as a sign. He likened the words and deeds of humankind to fruit when he exhorted us to bear good fruit. Going deeper into the metaphor, his sober words spelled out that a good tree could not bear bad fruit or a bad tree good fruit. Jesus, in Matthew's Gospel, said that it would be by our fruits that we would be known.*

St Paul, keen to get us away from thinking about ourselves as subject to law, to the appeasement of a vengeful God by good deeds, spelled out to the Church in Galatia the virtues that would characterise a Christian. And the fruit of the Spirit would be love, joy, peace, patience, kindness, goodness, faithfulness, gentleness, and self-control.

Before exploring St Paul's argument further, we should note that the phrase he uses is 'fruit of the Spirit' and not 'fruits of the Spirit'. In some translations of the Bible, the word 'harvest' is used. The harvest of the Spirit is one harvest, one fruiting, and each of the nine virtues is a sign of the whole fruiting. Each has its own unique characteristics but all are interdependent, as we will see when we come to contemplate them one by one. For this reason, I will use the word 'fruit' when referring to the whole fruit of the Spirit, but will refer to the component parts as 'virtues'.

* Matthew 7:20

Returning to St Paul, the manifestation of this spiritual fruit would testify to the quality of the tree that bears it. The tree is the family tree of God's descendants, both those of the original genus, like God's ancient people the Jews who had become Christians, and those who were grafted on by the grace of God, the gentile converts to Christianity. We are to understand that fruit-bearing Christians would be signs of the kingdom of God, their virtue the manifestation of that kingdom.

If we have any humility at all, at this point we remember how little we manifest virtues of love and joy, how little peace we know and show, how often we are not gentle or patient or kind or good or faithful, how often we are out of control. We confess, with monotonous regularity, our catalogue of sins and shortcomings. But if we are not careful, we begin to lose sight of something very important.

Much of the fruit today is bought in a supermarket. In order for the fruit to qualify for a place on the shelves it must pass stringent tests. On display, fruit must not have too many blemishes or bruises. A brown spot on a banana and it is removed from the shelf and destroyed. A worm-hole in an otherwise sound apple means the apple will not be displayed or sold.

When Jesus plucked a fig from the tree to illustrate his point about us bearing good fruit,* that fig is unlikely to have been good enough for the supermarket shelf. It may well have had a hole in it, a blemish. It may have been small and a bit dried up, but, as far as Jesus was concerned, it was good fruit. A banana with a brown spot on it is still a good banana! Less than perfect fruit is good fruit too and is picked from the tree and sold in many different markets throughout the world. Keep this in mind as we now consider each virtue in turn.

* Matthew 7:20

Focus for reflection

. . . you will recognise them by their fruit.
Matthew 7:20

Group activity

Ask each group member to read the introduction before the first session. Ask them to bring with them a piece of fruit that they feel symbolises their own character or personality. Assemble the pieces of fruit in a bowl and make it the focal point of the room. Ask group members to share the reason for their choice of fruit as a way of introducing themselves to the rest of the group. An alternative approach might be for group members to share their choice of fruit with a partner before adding their fruit to the bowl as they are introduced by their partner to the rest of the group.

Chapter One

Self-control

For this exploration of the nine-fold fruit of the Spirit, I have drawn upon the metaphor of a beautiful place with views into the distance, but with an upwards slope that is sometimes challenging. It is a place with twists and turns and unexpected vistas. Perhaps it is like a national park or a botanical garden. I hope that we may take our time on the journey, resting here and there to consider and to contemplate.

I am reminded of a visit to a beautiful botanical garden on the island of Madeira. The advertisements for this attraction promised much and I was not disappointed. The only problem I had was in locating the entrance to the garden. Finding the way in was a frustrating and a taxing exercise, but once I had found the entrance I was instantly restored.

Something of this difficult experience came to mind as I pondered on the virtue of self-control. Having resolved to reverse the order of the virtues listed by St Paul, I was half-wishing I had not done so because this virtue seemed to be too much of a challenge at this stage. I found it difficult to find the way into it.

My hypothesis is that where we find virtue we find something of God. Contemplating God as Love or as Peace seems easier than contemplating God as Self-control. I wrestled with a number of concepts, trying a number of 'gates' to gain access to this virtue. In doing so, I was reminded of a mathematics teacher who would set a problem for his pupils to solve but would insist that all the 'workings out' were included in the answer. What follows is not only the conclusion I came to, but my 'workings out'.

St Paul tells us that self-control is a virtue,* but it could be perceived, in reality, to be a disabling self-obsession that distances us from God by shunning his influence upon our life. Alternatively,

* Galatians 5:23

self-control might be necessary to good health – for example, having the self-control not to put one's hand in a fire, and so causing serious self-harm. I remember nursing a woman who had burned her hand whilst suffering an epileptic fit. She was injured because her hand was not under her control at the time. Here we find that self-control, as a sign of healthy living, may not be virtuous as such, and yet having the freedom to thrust a hand into the fire to rescue someone also calls for self-control and could be regarded as virtuous. The effect might be the same as in the first example, when a hand thrust into the fire occurred because of a lack of self-control, but the latter incident might be considered selfless and heroic. We might then understand the virtue of self-control as an attribute of human behaviour that is essential to healthy living and growth towards wholeness, but which is normally exercised freely and with conscious will.

In some circumstances, then, we might admire a degree of self-control. Virtues are admired in other people, though we may be rather self-effacing about them in ourselves. The self-control exercised by the gymnast, the tightrope walker, or the 'slimmer of the year' may fill us with admiration. Conversely, if we are not athletic, have a poor sense of balance or are overweight, we may behold self-control in others with a degree of self-loathing. We might ask ourselves why it is that self-control has a bad press in some quarters and yet is valued in others.

How difficult it seems to be to get the balance right. Perhaps the problem lies in what we believe about God. Is God in control and does he expect his Church to exercise control on his behalf? Let us explore further what we might mean by self-control.

Self-control has been called Governance.* It can be likened to someone who steers a boat, who has a gentle hand on the tiller and guides the boat along. But it verges on obsessiveness and narrowness when it is like a person who steers the boat by setting the oar in the water but who never moves it in response to changing tides or winds so that the boat moves them in the right direction.

* I am indebted to the Revd Professor J. M. G. Williams of the University of Wales, Bangor, for help in the use of this term.

Self-control requires a degree of self-knowledge, of self-perception, and is exercised in a spirit of compassion and kindness towards oneself, along with some awareness of what is going on around us.

People get themselves into emotional knots and feel out of kilter, out of control. What they lose is the ability to self-monitor: to know what is happening, objectively, around them – to ask, 'What's going on?' They lose the ability to know what they know. This degree of self-awareness is well developed in human beings, but if we lose the ability to self-evaluate – to assess ourselves but without judging ourselves – we may be unhealthily out of control. Although comparisons of ourselves with other people can also be unhelpful, it is our very ability to compare ourselves with others, and with ourselves in other circumstances, that helps us to monitor the acceptability of our behaviour. Clearly, we learn very early on what behaviour is acceptable behaviour, say, at a football match compared with that at a funeral service. Additionally, allowable behaviour is culturally based. We could contrast acceptable behaviour at a dance with acceptable behaviour in church until we remember that liturgical dance is a feature of some Christian worship.

If we lose self-control, we might also lose the ability to self-reward. We might no longer be able to give ourselves a reward or to congratulate ourselves. It can be argued that our aim is to be so God-centred that we hand over all 'control' to him and, along with it, any desire to congratulate or reward ourselves: seeking to snatch nothing back from God. If we do that, we may abdicate all responsibility for our own behaviour; we may even blame God for any consequent behaviour: 'I am not in control of myself; God is in control and he told me to do this.'

In the foothills of virtue, which, we hope, will lead us to the higher plains of virtue, we may find it difficult to gain access. This virtue of self-control can seem so complex and confusing. Already we have considered it as a contextual virtue (remember the act of thrusting a hand in the fire, either involuntarily or to rescue another). Self-control as governance may seem a long way from our own experience of self-control, or our own conditioned thinking. It may help us to think of self-control as associated with the taking of responsibility for our actions.

Here we might come close to St Paul's intention. Translated sometimes as 'temperance',* the virtue of self-control takes on a corporate as well as an individual meaning. More often than not, the behaviour of one person affects the behaviour of others, but quite often we hear of individual behaviour without regard or care for the consequences for other people as being a virtue in itself. Being 'my own person' can sometimes mean 'behaving how I like regardless of how it affects other people'.

There is, too, a human tendency to want to control other people. Such behaviour has more to do with power than a desire to enhance the quality of human life. Sadly, the one can easily masquerade as the other. Relationship counsellors often encounter situations in which someone has dominated the behaviour of another – perhaps preventing them from leaving their home, or seeing friends – and has claimed that all was done for the welfare and protection of the partner.

Many people regard Christians as odd or over-controlled because some aspects of Christian lifestyle are in contradiction to their own, but is this accusation fair? Some Christians make their life-style a banner of their faith and sometimes it is the lifestyle that people recall, admire or ridicule; the Christian teaching that spawned the lifestyle being misunderstood or forgotten. To complicate matters further, those who choose a lifestyle in response to a certain teaching of the Christian faith can themselves forget the purpose behind the teaching and make a religion or a god out of their lifestyle choices. The code of behaviour assumes an importance above and beyond the tenet of faith on which it was based. Jesus recognised this phenomenon and spoke out against it. He warned the Pharisees of the dangers of keeping the many rules that governed their daily life whilst forgetting the central teaching of the Law of Moses and of the Law of Love.

In the ministry of spiritual guidance or direction, one comes across people who are being spiritually 'strangled' by their own 'rule of life'. It may be a rule of life that had been suggested to them many years before when a certain kind of structure to their

* Authorised Version of the Bible

prayer time might have been welcome and helpful. For some people, the regimen had become a familiar habit that was not harmful but not helpful either; but, for others, the keeping of the rule, to the letter, had become a life-draining obsession.

I referred earlier to St Paul's use of the expression 'self-control', calling it a sign of the fruiting of the Holy Spirit in us. Returning to the translation as 'temperance', we may find, in the life of the early Church, clues to the out-working of this virtue in individuals and in communities.

Christian communities were often quite small and met discreetly. They lived a quiet life. St Paul himself had urged them not to make a spectacle of themselves but to blend in as much as their conscience would allow: to be the leaven in the lump. They were not to draw attention to themselves. In sharing the Gospel they were simply storytellers. If people thought there was something different about their behaviour, it would be because they were exhibiting Christian virtues of love and joy and peace.

St Paul also urged people not to be gluttons and to exercise self-control because they lived in communities who shared all they had together. With the obvious exception of family life, very few Christians in our generation live that way. We make modest contributions to the life and work of the Church, but many of us hold ourselves fairly peripheral to the church community. For most of us, our contribution is only a token, a gesture, towards communal living. But in the early Church, anyone who took more than their fair share of the communal food or other resources would have been depriving a brother or sister of what they needed in order to live.

As people become more individualistic, the community effect can be harder to identify. We have all met those who, at a Christian social gathering, sit themselves near the food and systematically eat their way across the table. Someone organising a church tea told me how the tea had to be 'plated up'; otherwise some people would grab the lot and even stuff food into their pockets or hand-bags. I thought she was exaggerating until I saw a huge piece of chocolate cake being wedged into a very small handbag!

Paul's purpose was not to take all the fun out of life but to ensure that the small and vulnerable Christian communities did not lay themselves open to unnecessary difficulties. In pagan societies, where drunken orgies were common, these new Christians could make themselves vulnerable by being intemperate or 'out of control'. Drunken carousing would also have drawn unwanted attention to themselves.

From time to time, in the history of the Christian Church, this virtue, translated as temperance, has come to be associated almost exclusively with total abstention from alcohol. Although such temperance has made a valid statement in society, there have been occasions when it has been over-emphasised at the expense of other godly virtues and has simply served to make Christian living appear 'freaky' to non-believers, to the point where sharing our faith, in any meaningful way, is put beyond our reach.

It is not, of course, only Christians who suffer from social pressure to conform to the lifestyle choices of others. Those who abstain from drinking alcohol as a matter of personal choice, or for health, safety or economic reasons, as well as for religious reasons, can be judged unfairly in a society where the majority of adults drink alcohol. They can be made to feel like freaks. This does nothing to help the recovering alcoholic, the driver, or the religious abstainer.

Christian self-control can seem to be more about living according to a set of rules. St Paul was trying to distinguish how Christians, living in the freedom of the Spirit of God, should behave, as distinct from others. His point is that self-control is the fruit of living appropriately and comes out at the end of the process of Christian nurture: rather like the apple is the end of a process that starts with the blossom in the spring. Self-control, temperance, moderation in all things, living responsibly, are hallmarks of a life lived within the freedom of the Spirit of God and have little to do with dogged adherence to laws of restraint. Self-discipline is a partner with the grace of God.

There is a fine balance between exercising self-control and controlling the way other people live. Obvious ways include telling people what they should wear or eat, or how they should behave. There are subtle ways, too, by which people manipulate others, like the floor covering in department stores, which is designed to either speed the customer through an area or to slow them down in the hope that they will take a closer look at the merchandise on offer. When self-control is considered as taking responsibility for others and ourselves, the situation is rather different. Having a route marked to speed customers out of the department store in the event of fire is a sign of taking responsibility for a controlled and safe evacuation.

When it comes to being a control freak, it could be said that the Church is the expert. In the name of God, the Church has been telling people how to live their lives for two thousand years. Again, there is a difference between taking responsibility, under God, for leading people towards God, and taking from people their freedom of choice. Isn't this the difference between being a church and being a cult?

If we think of God as being a controller, we fly in the face of the free will he has given us. God is no puppeteer who moves us across the stage of life, lifting our feet, one in front of the other, by hidden strings, and yet there is something very reassuring, something deep inside us that knows that there must be a reason and a purpose for what happens to us. We might have sensed God's hand gently guiding us. We may have looked back over our life and been able to discern how he rescued us from this or led us toward that. Surely we need to believe that someone or something has the master plan and can make sense of all we see, experience or suffer?

Perhaps we have travelled further into the foothills of virtue than we had thought, encouraged by a sign that says, 'Responsibility taken here.' Perhaps the virtue of 'self-control' is that of 'taking responsibility'. God took upon himself the responsibility of rescuing us from spiritual death by sending Jesus that we might have life.* Jesus is the responsible King who 'bowed his head and gave up his spirit'[†] in the most responsible act of all. God the Father took on the responsibility of raising Christ to new life,[‡] making it possible for humankind to be restored: to become like Christ.

* John 10:10   † John 19:30   ‡ Romans 6:4

So, we begin to see that as we become more virtuous, more like Christ, we exercise more responsibility for ourselves, for each other, for our environment. We promote God's life-giving and liberating message by encouraging others to take more responsibility for how they live. We begin to understand something quite crucial: that every responsible act by humankind reveals a little more of the responsible God.

Taking responsibility for ourselves following a major health crisis or a bereavement, for instance, can be a long, slow and painful process. Any situation in which our self-confidence is undermined leaves us weakened and vulnerable. With help, and the right kind of support and encouragement, we begin to take control. This takes nothing from God. The more we become responsible, the more we manifest the responsible God. As healthy self-control is restored, we begin to manifest virtue: we recover sight of the God who has taken responsibility for restoring all his creation, working wonderfully through us and through those around us. In this, God makes himself present in an awesome way, leaving no doubt who is in charge, whose hand is on the tiller.

Isaiah prophesied the coming of a Saviour: 'And the government shall be upon his shoulders and he will be called: Wonderful Counsellor, Mighty God, Eternal Father, Prince of Peace . . .'* His words come so close to our understanding of self-control as responsible kingship. They might have read: 'and the *governance* shall be upon his shoulders'. Every tiny step taken by those recovering God-given governance reveals the King of glory.

The paradox of discipline, responsibility and self-control, and the knotty problem of how to set people free to walk their own pilgrimage towards God, continue to challenge us. We continue to learn from God how to encourage and support people, without trying to control them, as we discover the responsible God in others and learn from them. At last we are on our way into the hinterland of virtue, the difficult entry forgotten.

* Isaiah 9:6

Focus for reflection

Jesus said, 'If you stand by my teaching, you are truly my disciples; you will know the truth and the truth will set you free.'
John 8:32

Group activity

Using a large round tray as a base, each bring a contribution to the building of a 'hill of virtue'. This might comprise stones, gravel, soil, sand and plants, rather like an Easter garden. Light a small candle or tea light for each virtue, adding one more each week as the virtues are discussed and the 'hill' builds.

Questions for discussion

1. To what extent do you think God controls the details of your life?
2. What areas of life are out of control?
3. How do we help people to take responsibility for themselves?

Suggestions for prayer

Lord,
you are the supreme Governor
and the whole universe belongs to you;
and yet you do not work me like a puppet.
Thank you for setting me free to respond to you in love.
Amen.

Lord,
you have taken responsibility for all your people.
Thank you for calling me to share in that responsibility
by helping me to be responsible for how I live and behave.
Amen.

Lord,
you know me so well
and know the areas where I am out of control.
Help me to feel your gentle but firm hand
on the tiller of life, over my shaky hand.
Help me to steer a course straight to the heart of your love.
Amen.

Chapter Two

Gentleness

Some biblical translators have used the words 'humility' and 'meekness' rather than gentleness to name this virtue. Continuing to explore our hypothesis that God is made manifest and contemplated in human virtue, we might find it difficult to think of God as meek and humble until we have met him in Jesus Christ who humbled himself and took upon himself our nature. We call God 'Almighty' and we recognise his power, but can he be both all-powerful and all-gentle? It was with this question in mind that I came to reflect on what I have come to understand as the paradox of strength and gentleness. As I tested my theory that all true human virtue is a manifestation of God himself, I searched for an understanding of gentleness and true humility as being something strong. The image came to mind of Jesus before Pontius Pilate. He was virtually silent, yet his strength intrigued Pilate. When Jesus spoke, his words carried authority and strength. He spoke with meekness and humility. The gentleness of his words moved Pilate, but their power unnerved him.*

A few years ago, I settled myself in our conservatory to ponder on the subject of gentleness. What my wife and I called the conservatory was really a rather rickety glass and aluminium-framed lean-to, but with a rug or two and a couple of chairs it had become a pleasant little place to think. It stood on a good concrete base and concrete had been laid in a border around the outside to encourage rainwater to run away and into the garden. The concrete border was about 30 centimetres wide. Wear and tear and countless winter frosts had caused the concrete to crack. It wasn't meant to last for ever and it became less serviceable as time went by. Lily of the valley plants had forced their way up through the cracks in the concrete and made a cheerful show in the spring.

* John 19:8

There were so many of them that they had widened the gaps in the concrete and had displaced some of the pieces. One rarely thinks of lily of the valley as strong and yet they are very sturdy little plants with strong stems and strong broad leaves. In the centre is a stem with delicate bell-like flowers. They also have a delicate scent. They were my inspiration for writing about strength and gentleness.

It seems to me that many hold the philosophy that the way to get things done in this life is to be strong; to be solid in one's opinion and to focus on the goal regardless of any obstacles. We have all met machismo people who believe that the only real way to achieve anything or to reach any goal is to bully and brow-beat their way through the crowd. I am referring to people in every walk of life, including Christian ministers who have found that their behaviour is effective and that effectiveness becomes the justification for what they do. Sometimes we may not have the personal resources to resist tyranny and brow-beating. Indeed, the more we are beaten, the less we might feel able to resist.

Some people, motivated by the highest ideals, have argued that brow-beating, harassing and tyrannising people is the only way to make things happen, even good and acceptable things. In many instances their behaviour is an abuse of power.

I knew one parish priest who deliberately bullied everyone from the altar servers to the quiet and harmless soul who came to the early service to say her prayers. He claimed that he deliberately made aggressive telephone calls to those from whom he required some action, claiming that this always got him what he wanted. In his own defence he said that he always rang back the next day to apologise for losing his temper. He admitted that relationships were tested to the limit but he found they were soon restored. The main thing was that his outburst resulted in his achieving his objective, yet it was difficult to see Jesus in such behaviour.

Those who treat us like that rarely see the need to adopt a different approach to suit the circumstances. As a consequence, we may be overwhelmed. David Ford in his book *The Shape of Living** considers modern-day 'overwhelmings'. His expression

* *The Shape of Living,* David F. Ford (Fount)

describes the feelings so well. Ford, being positive, encourages us to find ways to adjust to these overwhelmings. He recognises that we cannot always hope to eradicate them. It is like the ocean. We cannot eradicate the waves but we can surf the waves as best we can. Even if we are overwhelmed by water, one can either drown or learn to swim under water, coming up for air now and again.

Consider my lilies of the valley and how they have pushed aside the concrete pieces to stand erect and cheerful; to give delight to the senses. Where there is a crack in the solid and offending concrete, they find a way through and then slowly expand the space, finding themselves some elbow room, some space to breathe and to grow. They have learned to adapt to their environment.

Power comes in different guises. There is the power of authority which enables one to make something happen because those under authority are duty-bound to obey, or because they fear the consequences of disobedience. There is the power of influence; that is, the ability to sell an argument or to persuade others to one's own point of view. It is a power base that relies on personality, charisma and charm to win others round. There is the power of expertise whereby a lead is followed because one has specialist knowledge or skill on which others rely. A combination of these can be a potent cocktail of power that is lethal in the wrong hands.

In the face of such abuse of power we may ask ourselves, 'How can the meek (or the gentle) inherit the earth?'[*] The answer may lie in another power base altogether: the power of disclosure. By this I mean the power that comes from being prepared to be open and vulnerable. It is the confrontation of the enemy with weapons of patience, kindness, generosity and sincerity.

As Christians, we are to model ourselves on Christ and Christ alone, and there is no room for power games of our own. Stories abound about disputes within the Church. The display of fierce argument, bitterness and prejudice can be a public display of

* Matthew 5:5

scandal. If such scandal sets a single questioning or searching person back, even one step, on their pilgrimage towards God, then we should feel ashamed. Whatever the outcome, the image of the Church is tarnished, and the kingdom of God is set back. The enemies of God, once again, point a finger of scorn and treat the Church with contempt. Better, surely, to demonstrate our ability to discuss and debate and to reconcile our differences in a truly Christian way: a truly gentle way that will make people marvel at a God who can do this in us. The gentleness of God will be revealed and others will be drawn to him.

The gentle 'lily' approach to our problems takes patience and time, and there is a great temptation to shovel on the concrete of self-opinionation. We have, too, the story from St Matthew's Gospel* of how Peter, James and John had come down from the mountain to the real world in which the forces of darkness are pitted against the forces of light. Their own inadequacy is used as an illustration of the power of God in Jesus, and the question about their own ability to act with his authority leads to the teaching of Jesus on the need for prayer, not just prayer of authority and confidence, but deep prayer that is a way of life and is about relationship with God: prayer of being, and not just prayer of doing. Elsewhere, when disputes arose among the disciples, Jesus would turn convention on its head and teach humility and servanthood.[†]

We promote the kingdom of God not by laying down the law, nor by bullying or threat, nor by blackmail, bribery or inducement, but by revealing God-like behaviour. This is not to say that we will avoid issues or be unable to stand firm when we need to. We must not confuse gentleness with acquiescence or submission. Sometimes we must speak out as the prophets of old spoke out. They were not always gentle in their delivery and neither was Jesus. To some extent gentleness is assertiveness. We hope for a resolution that has a God-givenness about it. We seek a resolution to conflict that God has designed and one in which all parties have been built up and the kingdom of God forwarded.

A bullish approach affects not only our behaviour towards others

---

* Matthew 17:1-8   † John 13:3-17

but our behaviour towards God. We have all heard God bullied in prayer and have heard Christians in prayer huddles psyching themselves up like an American football team huddled together to agree strategy, or like Maori warriors preparing for battle. Often what is needed is not endless, wordy, clenched-fist and muscular prayer, but deep sighs of prayer that draw us to the gentle heart of the Father for our refreshment, strengthening and empowering. Sometimes, to find God in prayer, we need to go through a very small door marked 'Meekness' or 'Humility'. Like Alice in Wonderland we need to be small enough to get through it. When we find and touch the gentleness within us, we find the small door and we can pass through quite easily.

People with the capacity to be gentle, some of the time, can learn to use their gift effectively, pragmatically and economically. We all have the potential to be 'concrete' or to be 'lily'. Sadly, we may have learned that our gentleness is considered as weakness and we may try to hide it.

Consider John who had a senior management post in a large paper manufacturing company. He responded to a call to ordained ministry and was accepted for training. He had a reputation for being outspoken, opinionated, even aggressive in his behaviour. For all that he was a likeable fellow and people forgave him his outbursts. This did not prevent him from having further outbursts of inappropriate behaviour, and one began to fear for those to whom he would minister. In his defence, he had adopted behaviour that was typical of the culture in which he had worked. That was no real excuse for the way he could behave, although some might say that he was simply being himself and that he had integrity. There was something else about him, something that was equally 'him', something that was quite hidden. One saw it for a second and then it was gone. It was gentleness.

I said to him one day, after one of his outbursts, 'John, I think you are terrified that people will find out about your gentle nature.' He looked at me in absolute amazement and told me that his wife had been saying that to him for years. He admitted that he needed help in accessing his gentle nature. He was afraid that his gentleness would be interpreted as weakness. He had not discovered the power of disclosure but perhaps, in his admission, he was beginning to discover it. I shared with him a quotation that means a lot to me. It is from St Francis de Sales, who is credited with saying, 'Nothing is so strong as gentleness; nothing is so gentle as real strength.'

Christians are not an oppressed minority, even though we might feel that we are. Everything that was available from God to the early Christians is available to us. In addition, we have the experience of our forebears, their triumphs and their failures, to help us along. The promise of God is that he will protect us with the armour of his Spirit, and that all his will is achievable through us, and by his grace.

There is something here for us about knowing the God we worship, revealed in Jesus Christ, and about knowing ourselves. We need to know what is strong in us and what is delicate. It is the difference between the strong stem of the lily of the valley and its delicate scent. We are both, but we need to learn to use appropriate behaviour.

My suggestion is that if we try our best to behave appropriately, and admit our shortcomings, we will be more effective in building the kingdom of God than if we are headstrong megalomaniacs. We hear many assertions to the contrary: 'I am what I am'; 'Take me or leave me'; 'If they don't like my style, then tough luck!' Of course we are who we are, and we are not perfect, but it is more a matter of who we might become by the transforming grace of God.

Looking for the lily of the valley among us takes a little more effort. By virtue of their style, the lilies among us do not stand out from the crowd. They say little at meetings but when they speak, people listen. They work quietly, effectively and humbly for the kingdom of God. Such people are strong and gentle.

According to St Paul, gentleness is part of the fruit of the Spirit.* Like market gardeners we have to be philosophical about the fortunes of the harvest. When there is an abundance of fruit, they rejoice. When there is little, they are thankful for what they

* Galatians 5, 22-23

have. So it is with us. Sometimes there is more evidence of the fruit of the Spirit in our lives than at other times. We are eternally grateful for the fruit produced because even the poorest harvest is a sign of God's bountiful Spirit at work in us. So it is with gentleness. We know that some people seem more gentle than us; gentleness seems to come naturally to them. Others of us must be grateful for what gentleness there is. We hope that through prayer and discipline we will yet bear a fuller harvest. We should be aware, too, that scourging and scolding ourselves because we have not been gentle compounds the offence because we fail to be gentle with ourselves.

In the Book of Genesis we read how we were created in the image and likeness of God.* We were glowing: perfect creations of our loving creator God. We know that however hard we try, the reality is that we are far from that perfect image. We may conclude that we are tarnished, damaged, broken specimens of humanity, that we have lost something of our value because of that. As they would say on a certain television antiques show, 'If it were in perfect condition it would be worth a fortune, but, as it is, with that chip or crack in it, with the lid missing and only one leg – well, fifty pence at a jumble sale.' What a depressing thought!

It is all too easy to note the times that we weren't gentle. It is all too easy to mistake true humility for self-effacement. It is difficult to receive a compliment without protest, and to face the truth about ourselves especially when the truth is that God has been glimpsed in us! It can be a harder discipline to accept a compliment than to dwell on our worthlessness. Although such dwelling has been a means of inspiration for many, it doesn't work for me! All it does for me is to feed my low self-esteem and undermine my confidence. The devil knows just when to whisper in my ear, 'You, you're worth nowt!'

But then we remember God's redeeming grace that can transform us but not back to our original undamaged selves. If we use a model of our redemption that is about putting things back the way they were, we go against every other law of both the natural

* Genesis 1:27

and the spiritual realm. If we look for a restoration of innocence, we deny experience, and life experience has taught us so much. God does not put things back the way they were. He has moved on and so must we. Everything in scripture tells us so. When Jesus healed and restored people, those he touched were not the same as they had been before they had succumbed. Now they were filled with something new and positive and dynamic that sent them skipping off in joy and praise.

What we are, and what we have become, remain 'us' throughout. 'What we shall be,' as St Paul says in his letter to the Romans, 'is yet to be revealed in us.'* What it clearly won't be is a restoration to the original. The activity of the Holy Spirit in our lives, the partnership of activity between us and God, has meant that God, who made us in his image and likeness, is taking our broken component parts and is making something new. Out of every episode of inappropriate behaviour (call it sin, if it helps) God takes our experience and transforms it through forgiveness and healing and makes something new of it. What we are becoming is yet more wonderful. What God can make of us is too wonderful to contemplate. As we become more like Christ, we reveal the strong gentleness of God. As our eyes and ears are opened by God, we behold him in the gentle strength of others.

* Romans 8:18

Focus for reflection

Take my yoke upon you, and learn from me, for I am gentle and humble-hearted; and you will find rest for your souls.
Matthew 11:29

Group activity

- If the group members know each other well enough they might compliment each other in some way; responding to the compliment with a simple 'Thank you very much!'
- The ancients kept a human skull near them to remind them of the fragility of life. Group members may like to keep a fresh egg near them for the time between group sessions and share, next time, their reflections upon it.
- Make a collage of examples from nature of gentleness combined with strength.

Questions for discussion

1. In your experience do the meek really inherit the earth?
2. Should Christians be assertive?
3. Do you ever bully God?

Suggestions for prayer

Lord,
I am not always gentle with myself or with others.
Sometimes, through frustration, impatience,
or zeal for your kingdom,
I bully people.
I even bully you
when I want a swift answer to my prayers.
Teach me, Lord, to be gentle with people,

so that I do not obscure their view
of your gentleness and strength.
Amen.

We praise you, Lord,
for the way you reveal yourself in virtue.
Forgive the times when I have not recognised you
in the gentleness of others.
Amen.

Chapter Three

Faithfulness

We begin to make promises when we are very young. We promise not to run out into the road. We promise to eat up all our vegetables. We promise to keep our bedroom tidy. We also begin to break promises at a very early age. The scolding by an anxious parent as we are yanked back on to the pavement, the cold, untouched cabbage and the mountain of bedroom debris all testify to our inability to keep promises. The wonder of it is that we are no less loved because of it. In asking us to promise this or that, the loving parent anticipates a less than perfect response. The words 'We'll see!', in response to our sincere and good intentions, testify to the wisdom and experience of the parent who has made and broken similar promises in their time.

There is an understanding that we need to make allowances for immaturity, but when are we mature? St Paul suggests that maturity comes only when we measure up to the fullness of the stature of Christ. On the one hand, we could despair of ever being like Christ and be overwhelmed by a sense of inferiority, or we can relax into the human state and remind ourselves that we are human, imperfect and faithless, but that God loves us just the same.

I heard the story of a man who prayed to God, 'Father, forgive me the sins of my youth.' God replied, 'The sins of your youth! Why would I recall the sins of your youth when you were faithless but knew no better? Rather it is the sins of your old age that bother me: the times when you stand in judgement of others who have been no more faithless than you were.'

Some of the promises we make are more serious and the breaking of them may have dire consequences; others are less significant. The child may run into the road with tragic consequences. We may survive not eating cabbage. But, as we grow up, we are expected to take more responsibility for the promises we make. As the young adult leaves home, he promises to write every week. If he doesn't write every week, but writes or calls sometimes, wise parents count themselves fortunate and they do not lambaste him because a letter hasn't dropped through the letter-box every Tuesday morning. As long as reasonable communication is maintained, the wise parent does not regard the promise as broken, and we may say that promises of that kind are insignificant when compared to solemn vows.

In addition to making many seemingly minor promises, many people do make solemn vows to God. Monks and nuns, for example, take vows of poverty, chastity and obedience. Priests and ministers take ordination vows. Wedding couples exchange solemn vows in the presence of God.

I have had the privilege of sharing in family milestone anniversary celebrations when couples have celebrated 25, 40, 50 and even 60 years of marriage. Gathered together are family and friends whose lives have been nurtured, touched and changed by the couple. Speeches testify to the good example the couple have been to everyone. Jokes, wry humour, and knowing looks disclose that life has not always been easy. Speech-givers gently allude to tragic losses, difficult times, disappointments, but none of these is allowed to steal the glory of the moment. People have not come to celebrate that life has been perfect, but that the couple have survived against the odds. Statistically, the chances of the marriage failing are quite high. Cynics might say that many couples would have lived more fulfilled lives had they parted years before. Not everyone sees it that way, and not everyone perceives themselves as free to make choices of that kind. Many people's relationships break up and they feel only pain and sadness, and because of this it can take huge effort to celebrate the lasting relationships of others.

Most people set out upon a relationship journey with expectations, hopes, and dreams. Declarations of love include pledges of total loyalty and self-sacrifice. All sincere and serious intentions are based in love. Love is the soil in which all virtue is rooted, but I am anticipating the final chapter of this book! It is as if our pilgrimage through virtue has brought us around another 'headland' and we have glimpsed our destination before our attention is brought back to the road beneath our feet.

We will consider love again, but here we consider the reality of human faithfulness. We consider it first as we observe human relationships before we contemplate faithfulness as an attribute of God to see if God is revealed in this virtue, glimpsed in all human faithfulness. The key question is this: Is God any less truly revealed just because human relationships are flawed?

Faithfulness is about relationships. Engagement rings, contracts and covenants are all outward and sacramental signs of promise. All are expressions of the God of faithfulness in whom all our promises are fulfilled.

Dare I say that no one keeps, perfectly, every promise or every vow that they make? In this sense we might call ourselves a faithless people. But every sincere attempt to keep a vow or promise, every New Year's resolution moment, is a pledge of intent that is not lost on a gracious and generous God who may well be saying to himself, 'We'll see!' with the same warm humour as the knowing and wise parent.

Such sincere pledges, such statements of good intent, rest in the faithfulness of God. They are (poor) reflections of the faithful God. The penitent who confesses that they have broken their Lenten promise, one day this year, needs to have their disappointment and regret taken seriously, but needs to be encouraged to celebrate the 39 days of Lent that they did not break their promise and to be sent on their way rejoicing in the love and grace of God.

Vows may be made for a moment in time; for 40 days or for life, but even as they are broken daily they are renewable daily.

Promises are made in relationship. They are also repaired, and renewed in relationship. Broken vows can only be redeemed by mercy and forgiveness, and they may only be transfigured and healed if we are given the opportunity to try to do better.

The way we keep, break, repair, renew and transfigure the promises and vows we make reveals the God of faithfulness to the world around us. When we celebrate our own successes, or those of others, we include the way we have worked through difficulties, through pain and tears, to a place of peace, mutual understanding, and a fresh start. We celebrate the Faithful God who, through the death and rising of Jesus, makes all fresh starts possible. For some, peace-making and mutual understanding may result in the setting aside of vows made and now unsustainable.

Consider Sister Mary who took life vows of poverty, chastity and obedience and sustained them for 23 years. The community to which she belonged had adapted and changed with the times and it had done that in order to survive. Mostly, Sister Mary had coped well with change. She had influenced some changes herself. But something else had changed – something deep inside Sister Mary, and something she found hard to articulate.

In recent years she had found herself increasingly out of step with the rest of the community. She tried hard to conform, to keep the spirit of obedience that had brought peace in the early days. Increasingly, she had begun to see herself, the community and the world about her in a very different light. Now, the keeping of the Convent Rule had become irksome, burdensome. Struggles with relationships within the community left her exhausted and drained of life. Vows that had once brought freedom to serve God unencumbered, she perceived as being barriers to the fulfilment of God's will for her. She had sought advice and help from her spiritual director as well as from her superiors in the community.

It was not that she was attracted by an alternative lifestyle. She was not seeking a personal relationship or a career. Indeed, should she leave the community at this stage, she would have little or nothing on which to rebuild her life. It would be easier, in some ways, to stay rather than to go. To settle for neither left her in limbo, a place where she could not be reached and rescued by anyone. To leave would be to set aside life vows, but to stay would be to live those vows without spirit. She would see her life as a hollow, meaningless, sham. She read the words, 'I came that they may have life, and may have it in all its fullness.'* She wondered just where that life was to be found.

Ultimately Sister Mary left the community, but not before she had become seriously depressed. In the end, it was the community,

* John 10:10

out of love, who encouraged her to leave. Their gifts to Sister Mary included not just clothes, money and a small apartment not too far from the Convent, but also a network of help and support. It was the community that did penance for this outcome, for not seeing how unhappy Sister Mary had become and how her life had ebbed in their presence. She had been emptied, and not in a poured-out and Christ-like way, but taken from her, making it harder for the God of faithfulness to reveal himself through her. Mary's rebirth and new life became a burning witness to the God of faithfulness and integrity; her renewed life, a source of life to others. Sometimes, giving each other the gift of liberation may be the only life-giving outcome.

Repentance, reconciliation, healing and renewal rarely mean a return to a former state. All human experience, including that of working through broken promises, changes us. We cannot be the same shape that we were before, but, by the grace of God, what we shall yet become may be more glorious, and may, ultimately, reflect more shiningly the glory of the God of faithfulness. All this is only possible because we have a God whose faithfulness never ends. It is not dependent on our poor attempts to be faithful to him. It is God who has taken the initiative, put out his faithful hand to us, and showed us a way to place our hand in his.

God entered into a lasting covenant with all his people. He sent his Son Jesus Christ, and sealed that covenant by his death on the cross and to rise again for us. He showed us a way of entering into the death and rising of Christ and called it baptism. By baptism, Christians become children of the promise: we have entered into an eternal covenant with God. This is the seal of God who promises to be faithful to us and the seal of our promise to *try* to be faithful to him.

We know, only too well, how easily we distance ourselves from the implications of this covenant. We are easily tempted to live in ways that are not worthy of our calling. Sometimes our habits, attitudes or behaviours betray how little we have responded to the goodness and faithfulness of God. Most of us are not unfaithful in hugely obvious ways. As we draw closer to an understanding of our baptism (a process that seems to take a lifetime), our consciences are honed and polished so that even little departures from God's code assume a greater significance.

Many of the saints of history interpreted temptation to sin as a sign of spiritual growth. The closer they were to living a faithful life, the more they might expect the powers of evil to try them. They saw such trials as a sign of growing in grace.

Here we might consider the nature of God's grace. The word 'grace' comes from the ancient Sanskrit and means two things at once: It is both the graciousness with which a thing is given or said, and the gratitude with which it is received. Graciousness and gratitude both come from the same root word and are like two ends of the same rainbow.

Looking at a rainbow may remind us of the story of Noah and of God's promise of faithfulness to his people.* It is a sign of the covenant, of the solemn promise made by God after the great flood that he would never again destroy his creation: 'This is the sign of the covenant that I make between me and you and every living creature that is with you, for all generations.' The righteous Noah had obeyed God's order to build an ark and to rescue enough living creatures to begin again after the destruction by the great flood.

Noah seems exemplary, and yet soon after becoming the first tiller of the soil, he showed his human fallibility. Growing vines in his newly tilled soil, he soon reaped a rich harvest and promptly got drunk from the wine that was produced! Lying naked in a drunken stupor, his family sought to cover him up and went to great lengths to avoid seeing him so exposed and vulnerable.

Awakening in great embarrassment, Noah cursed the one who had seen him naked, and set up a family rift among his descendants, the effects of which can be felt within the Jewish community to this day. The story may, of course, have been an attempt by the writer of the Book of Genesis to explain the tribal rift, but, taken on equal merit with the other stories in Genesis, it does demonstrate that although God had appeared to change his mind about his wayward people, his people had changed very little indeed! The

* Genesis 9:12-17

faithful God would have many an occasion to lament his people's failure to live up to their side of the bargain.

God was gracious in that he saved Noah and his family from destruction. Noah and his family responded with gratitude by trying to live a faithful life. God graciously promised never to destroy his creation again. But Noah's subsequent behaviour showed he was less than grateful to his gracious God. This is not to condemn poor Noah but to bring us a little comfort when we, too, behave no better. God loved Noah still and he loves us too!

Knowing that, or at least suspecting it, does not make temptation go away, but it may give us the incentive to try a little harder to resist it. Jesus, too, was tempted to sin, the first recorded incidence occurring in the desert soon after he was baptised in the River Jordan.* One of the differences between Jesus and us is that he did not break his promises, no matter how much he was provoked. He did not blame God for letting him down, as human beings so often do. Even on the cross, his cry of 'My God, my God, why have you forsaken me?' turns out to be a quotation from Psalm 22 that ends in an affirmation of faith and trust in God.

To be tempted is not the same as to sin. If we are not tempted to sin, then it may mean that we are spiritually dead. It may mean that the powers of evil have no need to go to work on us because we belong to them already. But if we are spiritually alive, then we can expect to be tempted.

It is so easy to attribute to God the very worst of human behaviour. We may suppose that God has given up on us in the way that fellow human beings have, or in the way that we have given up on ourselves. Conversely, when people have given up on God they sometimes look to their own resources to try to cope with their problems. This is not the same as taking responsibility for ourselves. Learning to accept help and support may be among the ways we allow God to help.

In the history of God's people, there have often been times when they were consumed by their own inward-looking notion of self-sufficiency. When they had force of arms, they were invincible.

* Mark 1:9-11

When their crops failed and they had no bread, they turned to the Lord in shame and guilt, and called upon him to save them. It would seem that people haven't changed very much. When they feel strong, they seem to have no need of God. When things go wrong, it is God's fault for not stopping them from going wrong.

When we are less focused on God, less than faithful to him, we may become disorientated, uncoordinated; bumping around blindly. In this state we may find it difficult to see where to reach out for help. It is like trying to read signposts or to judge traffic when emerging from a crashed car with a head injury. In such circumstances, the chances of a second and perhaps worse injury are very high.

We may think of this effect of disorientation as a metaphor for personal spiritual difficulties, but when something similar happens on a societal or corporate level, the effect may be equally disastrous. When we begin to lose sight of what it means to be a faithful people, we may descend into wrangles and disputes that further fragment us. Perhaps Isaiah had something of this in mind when he urged God's people to stop galloping around like horses, to cease their endless plotting and scheming, and, once again, to put their trust in God. The prophet urged, 'In returning and rest you shall be saved; in quietness and trust shall be your strength.'* Returning to the crash victim analogy, it may be wiser to sit still on the pavement and to listen out for the sirens that herald rescue and help.

Paul, like Isaiah, calls upon God's people to show a little quiet trust, to put their trust in his strength and not in their own strength. God's people are still draining themselves in this way: their strength poured out in dissension, argument, plotting and rushing around in an uncoordinated fashion. But how are we to stop ourselves? How are we to become more focused, more faithful? Perhaps we have already discovered a possible answer in the previous chapter.

There comes a point – call it maturity if you like – when we have to take a little responsibility for the mess we make of our human relationships, for our broken promises. Taking responsibility,

* Isaiah 30:15

44

as we have already found, is at the heart of the virtue of self-control. Here, we have beheld the faithfulness of God who keeps his promises for ever. God has taken responsibility for us. We learn, sometimes painfully, to take some responsibility for our own behaviour. We learn to 'own up' to our broken promises and we learn, very slowly, to be compassionate towards others who are as faithless as we are. We learn to be compassionate towards ourselves. In so doing, we might find that the gentler approach to ourselves allows God to help us to be more faithful to him.

In this chapter we have contemplated the God of faithfulness and we have beheld him in all people of goodwill. We don't see rainbows every day, and sometimes, when we do, the colours are pale and indistinct, but they continue to testify to the indissoluble covenant between God and humankind, and are signs that none of the intentions behind our less-than-perfectly-kept promises are lost upon the God of Faithfulness.

Focus for reflection

Lord, your unfailing love reaches the heavens, your faithfulness to the clouds.
Psalm 36:5

Questions for discussion

1. Why do people find it so difficult to keep the promises they make?
2. Is a broken promise broken irrevocably, or can it be renewed daily?
3. Have you ever felt let down by God? If so, how?

Group activity

- Open a bottle of something sparkling (alcoholic or non-alcoholic!) and share a small celebration cake in honour of promises kept and vows sustained.
- Remember to add a little more to your garden of virtue and to light a candle for faithfulness.

Suggestions for prayer

Lord,
we know you to be a faithful God
and ourselves to be a faithless people,
yet you love us still.
Help us to keep the promises we make to you,
to others, and to ourselves.
Amen.

Lord,
how easy it is to dwell upon our failings!
How easy it is to hear about the effects
that broken promises have made on the lives of others!
How easy it is to judge other people!
How much more difficult it is to celebrate
and to rejoice in lives lived out in faithfulness.
May the faithfulness we find in others
inspire and encourage us.
May we see you at work in our lives.
Amen.

Lord,
who alone can make all things new,
help those who seek a fresh start
to put behind them past failures,
and strengthen their resolve to be faithful to you.
Amen.

Chapter Four

Goodness

A preacher came to our church and began his sermon by asking the congregation if they were good. Only two people raised their hand. Unfortunately, they were my wife and me! The preacher was clearly embarrassed since the effectiveness of his next question depended on us seeing ourselves as less than good or not good at all. The matter was made worse for him because it was we who had asserted our goodness, thus seeming to undermine the preacher's authority to assert anything else. With a nervous laugh he said, 'Well, I suppose there is a theological basis for it (goodness).'

He recovered his composure, and, undaunted, he asked the members of the congregation to raise their hand if they had ever done anything naughty or wrong. Everyone, including my wife and me, raised a hand. The preacher was then able to make his point that we have all sinned and fallen short of the glory of God* and that we are all in need of the saving grace of God, achieved for us by the death on the cross of our Lord Jesus Christ.

I have no quarrel with his assertion. What exercised me was the contrast between being 'good' and being a sinner. If the preacher had asked us to raise a hand if we thought we were perfect, I have no doubt that there would not have been a hand to be seen. It would follow, then, that all hands would be raised to own up to having done something 'naughty' or 'wrong'. His central point would have been made equally well but without leaving the large and family-orientated congregation in doubt about something essential and valuable about themselves.

The issue is whether or not we are basically good. On that will depend whether we can behold goodness in someone, and whether, or not, that goodness is a glimpse of God who is good.

* Romans 3:23

Someone once asked Jesus what good deed he must do to have eternal life. Jesus rounded upon the person and asked another question by way of reply: 'Why do you ask me about what is good? One there is who is good. If you would enter life, keep the commandments.'*

The answer to the person's question about doing a good deed is in the end of the reply: 'If you would enter life, keep the commandments.' But Jesus' first and quick response is a fascinating and profound point about Good as noun, as God himself. After Jewish custom, the name of God is not used here, but 'One alone' cannot be considered to be anyone else but God.

If we start with the premise that God is good, we have a perspective on God as moral excellence. In accepting this premise we acknowledge that there is an objective moral excellence. We might find some comfort in the belief that God can name, label, describe and define morality, even if we find it hard to do so. We might find this helps us as we try to work our way through the complexities of modern living.

We hold that we are God's creation and that 'God saw everything he had made, and behold, it was very good.'† We hold, too, that we have a propensity to sin. We understand ourselves to have 'fallen' from this state of perfection and we know ourselves to be in need of God's saving grace. This does not mean there is no goodness in us. To deny that is to deny all that God is doing in us to restore us to his image and likeness.‡

In the face of so much that we might call less than perfectly good (I don't want to call it badness), we sometimes need help to recognise goodness in ourselves or in others: to see life through the eyes of people who have contemplated God in the goodness of others. If we imagine ourselves to be on a journey of discovery, seeking and finding virtue, we might be travelling in the company of others. As we walk, we might point out to each other places of special beauty or interest. In the same way, sometimes it takes others to help us to notice something truly wonderful in other people (or in ourselves): something that is a sign of the goodness of God.

* Matthew 19:16-17   † Genesis 1:31   ‡ Genesis 1:27

They are the people who can point to others and say to us, 'Behold, it is very good.'

One such person was Iris. Tiny and frail now as a result of a ravaging disease, Iris barely made an impression on the upholstery of a very large reclining armchair. She was comfortable, which was a blessing in itself. She hadn't always been so. Iris had been in constant pain. It was as if she had been locked in a cell with no window; she had no 'view' beyond her pain. Now, the combined art and science of medicine and nursing had brought about a sense of well-being that allowed her a little more independence and the clarity of mind to look around her again.

Within the year, Iris had lost her husband to a similar condition. She knew, only too well, the path the disease might take, but just for a while she had an opportunity to assess the value of her life. She named to me family members who were all loving and supportive. She named friends, neighbours, carers, and others who contributed to her sense of well-being.

Iris remarked that she had known many people in her life – 'some good, some not so good' – but only since she had been ill had she noticed how much goodness there was in people. By goodness she meant genuineness, gentle honesty, respect and integrity. She was amazed by the sheer volume of goodness that surrounded her, almost overwhelming her – a bit like the comfortable but enormous reclining armchair in which she rested.

She spoke of the chiropodist who always had a few minutes to stay and chat. She described each of her visitors to me, and identified how each brought some goodness to her through their purpose in coming but also through their ability to stay and listen and chat.

Some people are easier to stay with than others. Iris makes it easy to stay. Something of the goodness of God in her encourages one to stay. I am reminded of an expression picked up many years ago when I was training healthcare professionals in interpersonal relationship skills – 'You only get the behaviour you deserve.' The basic principle is that people will react to how we behave towards them. Approaching them with warmth, genuineness and unconditional positive regard is likely to encourage behaviour from them which is more helpful to both parties in solving a problem or a grievance. There is a mutuality of goodness and genuineness about Iris's relationship with people, and a recognition, by her and them, of something very good indeed. Surely, nothing short of God himself!

Genuineness! I am quite pleased with myself for spelling 'genuineness' correctly. When I write it on a flipchart pad it usually comes out like a famous Irish stout. The connection between 'goodness' and that same stout has long been exploited by its makers! 'Genuineness' has a Latin derivation and comes from the word for knee, with reference to a father acknowledging a new-born child by placing it on his knee. I am told that all newly born babies look like their father, so that the father will recognise the child as his own and will not reject it.

Jesus came to tell us that God acknowledges us as his children: he declares us genuine. In this sense we are intrinsically good but with a tendency to be less than perfect in our goodness. As Jesus said, 'One alone is good', but by God's acknowledgement we are 'of God' and, therefore, genuine. The degree of genuine goodness in us, at any one time in our life, is of secondary importance. It is also difficult for us to estimate or measure. We cannot take a kind of spiritual 'pulse' and ask ourselves, 'How good am I today?', like the jogger who stops every so often to take his pulse because a fitness manual has told him that, for his heart to keep healthy, he must achieve a certain pulse rate at least once a day.

Stripping away all that is false so that the genuine goodness of God in us can be revealed is a life-long process. It can be uncomfortable and costly. Alternatively, we can occupy ourselves with building up all kinds of facades because we fear there may be no genuine goodness in us at all!

There is a fashion in home decoration for creating 'faux' finishes. A variety of techniques are used to create the effect of tortoiseshell, marble or 'distressed' wood. My wife and I once attended a craft workshop where the participants were each given a small brown cardboard box. The craft teacher demonstrated how we would turn this rather plain and humble little box, by a technique called verdigris, into one which looked like brass or copper that had become tarnished by the elements.

We painted the box a turquoise colour and then dabbed on a copper coloured acrylic paint. Finally we rubbed a copper cream substance on to the corners and edges which we then buffed up. The effect was amazing, but I couldn't help being amused by the idea of making a cardboard box look like copper that had become tarnished; and I thought of my younger days when the pride of our street was shiny brass door furniture and a bright red polished doorstep. Everyone had brass ornaments on the mantelpiece and they had to be polished until they shone. 'Verdigris' was 'dirty-green' and a matter of shame!

I also thought of St Francis of Assisi. It was once said of him that he was sincere (*sans cère,* without varnish). He wasn't like the little box: dressed up to look like precious metal that has become tarnished. There was no varnish to disguise the cracks. He was the genuine article: no faux finish. The goodness of God shone through him. He wasn't perfect but he was being restored before the eyes of his contemporaries to the glory of God and to the encouragement of all his followers. Within the base cardboard box of his humanity was real preciousness – the presence of God – and that is what made him priceless. That is what makes us priceless. We have no need to be rubbed down or buffed up in order to be precious or to appear glorious. We need no faux finish to impress God, ourselves or each other.

In our own generation we have beheld the goodness of God shining through others, whether they be famous like Mother Theresa of Calcutta, or unknown to the world like Iris in her recliner. In them we see that goodness recognises goodness. Goodness reacts and responds to goodness, each in the other. This is the dynamic of God, who is good. Only God is good, but we are imperfect reflections of that goodness. To perceive goodness in another is to behold the genuine goodness of God, and it is beautiful to behold!

Having made the connection between goodness and genuineness, we may need to rest for a while to allow us time to take in the possibility that we are basically good because God is good and he has acknowledged us as his children, declaring us genuine.

Now we journey on a little further to consider the possibility that such goodness and genuineness gives us a kind of beauty.

Even though our image may be somewhat tarnished, we hold to the notion that God, in his goodness, is making something very beautiful and very precious in us. What is beautiful to God may not seem beautiful to us. What is beautiful to me, you may regard as ugly. We may not share another's opinion of beauty but aestheticians will assure us that there is an objectivity to beauty, but that our appreciation of that objectiveness is likely to be individual and subjective. What is beautiful and valuable; what is genuine and good seems so difficult to define.

Going into an art gallery one day, I saw clay pots of many kinds. I heard the gallery owner being asked what defined a pot as distinct from a sculpture. He said that anything with a hole in the top is a pot. Most pots have similar characteristics. There seems to be a firm base, a wide middle and a narrow neck! The narrow neck prevents liquids from evaporating too quickly and minimises contamination from outside by dust or flies. Clearly, there is a huge variety of pots. They have an authenticity as vessels that hold liquid, but each is different, individual. Whether or not they are beautiful to look at will depend upon how they are beheld, but, in their genuineness, they have an intrinsic beauty of their own, and in that beauty they reflect something of their maker. It is in making comparisons between people that we lose sight of objective beauty. All are being fashioned under the hand of the Divine Potter. All are unique and are becoming beautiful and stunning images of God.

Sometimes we do what the art gallery proprietor did with the exhibited pots: we put a value on each other. When asked how one compares exotic and unusual works of art (yet basically pots) with the more traditional handcrafted earthenware of the rustic cottage industry, he could not answer. The former were priced in hundreds of pounds, the latter available for just a few pounds. He struggled to say that all were beautiful in their own way. What he was able to say was that many items increased in value over the years. He showed examples of Victorian 'Pinkware' that could be found in many a home in Scunthorpe in the last century. Pots which were once bought for a few pence were now worth hundreds of pounds.

Some time ago, I spent a few days at the Convent of All Hallows on the Suffolk-Norfolk border. I have been there several times and I have never come away without a blessing. When I arrived, the guesthouse sister apologised because the chapel was in disarray. She lamented the temporary loss of what she described as their 'beautiful chapel'. To celebrate the centenary of the community, the nuns had decided to have the ceiling of the sanctuary repainted.

The chapel is Victorian and built in the High Church tradition. At the east end there is an apse and a high altar. The sanctuary is very ornate and gilded, decorated in the baroque style so beloved by the Victorians. High in the apse there is the painted ceiling. It is painted light blue with gold stars on it, symbolising, I think, the heavenly vault.

The next morning, two men were to start the work of repainting the ceiling which would take most of the week. I wandered into the chapel, mid-morning, to find the two men working quietly, talking in low voices whilst constructing a huge steel scaffold. The chapel echoed to the hammer blows as steel met steel and the structure grew taller and taller until it reached the painted 'sky' above.

It creaked and groaned as if in protest. A very ancient nun was sitting in a side aisle reading the Bible and she never moved a muscle. At first I admired her detachment and tried to emulate her, but then I let the building of the scaffold assault my senses.

I looked at the shiny steel bars which were straight and angular in contrast to the ornate carving and the baroque decoration. The loud hammering was in contrast to the gentle and slow tick of the clock that rules the day of these devoted souls. I heard the hammering and I thought of the soldiers nailing Love to the Cross. I thought of the applause in heaven, mingled with tears, as each blow was struck, as the moment of the salvation of the world drew near.

I listened to the creaks and groans of the structure, the murmurs of the men. They draped a rough and paint-stained cloth over the delicate reredos with such care. I thought of the lifeless body of Jesus lowered from the cross, and of the cloth in which he was so lovingly wrapped.

My thoughts stayed with that first Good Friday, with a scaffold built for the execution of offenders. We know that Golgotha, the place of the skull, was a permanent site for public execution, just outside the town. The scaffolding would have been permanently in place. It is likely that criminals carried only the huge cross beam to which they would be fixed before it was hauled into place by pulleys and ropes. Here, in this sedate and civilised chapel was the scaffolding, the pulleys and the ropes.

As the structure was being built I thought too of Jacob's ladder* that reached to the 'sky' above, and I thought of the permanent stairway to heaven that Jesus built by his death. The lifeless body of Jesus would be removed from the cross. The sacrifice – the one, true and only sacrifice – was complete, but the scaffold would remain. The ladder – the stairway, the structure of salvation – would be intact. Generation upon generation of Christians would be able to climb, to grow and to reach the top, and to touch the stars and to know the infinite love of God.

In that beautiful Chapel and in the beauty of the disarray and chaos, God's Spirit assaulted my senses and confronted me with the horror of the Cross. The ancient prayer of the Church came readily to me: 'We adore you, O Christ, and we bless you; because by your holy cross you have redeemed the world.' To me the chapel had never looked more lovely.

This unsuspecting tableau of the Passion against the backdrop of the artistry of the chapel forged a link. The goodness of God, through the Passion and death of Christ, restores humankind, once marred by sin and death, and gives it back an objectivity and a wondrous beauty.

* Genesis 28:12

Focus for reflection

Taste and see that the Lord is good. Happy are they who find
refuge in him!
Psalm 34:8

Questions for discussion

1. Do you think you are basically good, or basically bad?
2. How easy is it to know when people are genuine?
3. What is beauty, and how does it relate to goodness?

Group activity

Each group member will need a sheet of paper and a pen or pencil
to play this variation on an old parlour game.

Write your name at the top of the paper before passing the paper
to the person on your right. When you receive a piece of paper
from the person on your left, note whose name is at the top and
write a complimentary remark about them at the bottom of the
page. Fold up the bottom of the page to hide your comments and
pass the paper to the person on your right. Each time a paper
comes to you from the left repeat the exercise, remembering to
fold up the paper from the bottom to hide the compliment. When
you receive your paper back, unfold the paper to read the compli-
ments written about you. You may like to discuss them with a
partner.

Suggestions for prayer

Lord,
when you created the world
you looked upon all you had made
and saw that it was very good.
Look upon your people today and see your creation.
We believe we are precious in your sight.

Help us to silence the voices
that tell us we are of no real value;
that deny that your goodness dwells within us.
Amen.

Lord,
may our lives reflect your beauty and goodness,
and may we learn to recognise you
in the goodness we find in others.
Amen.

Lord,
thank you for the sacrifice of Jesus,
by which we can be restored to your image and likeness.
Amen.

Chapter Five

Kindness

Connie and Herbert were together for more than 40 years. They were well known in the village. They were sociable and outgoing, regularly going to dances in the village hall and other social events. When Connie died, following a long and painful illness, many people testified to her kindness. She was a good listener as well as having the knack of saying just the right thing to reassure or comfort. Many of her acts of kindness went unheralded but a neighbour volunteered how, one day, after she had received devastating news that had paralysed her family, she found a nourishing casserole on her back doorstep. It had been lovingly prepared by Connie and with it was a note that said, 'I didn't know what to say or what else to do.' The neighbour recalled that it was with the casserole in her hands, still warm from the oven, that she first began to believe that there just might be a God.

Some time later, during a discussion with a number of senior clergy, I used the phrase 'casserole evangelism'. Several of my colleagues scribbled it down. One asked me if it meant a kind of mixed approach to evangelism. I explained that I referred to an act of kindness that might raise in someone's mind the possibility of there being a God.

Connie was known for her kindness. She was a woman of faith, a regular at her local church, and everyone knew it. People had easily made the connection between her acts of kindness and her Christian belief.

Now Herbert was alone. More so because his old dog had had to be put to sleep. He told me that the vet had said it would be a kindness. Herbert looked directly at a photograph of Connie that was sitting on the mantelpiece, and then at me. The look said what he could not ask: 'Wouldn't it have been an act of kindness to have spared Connie so much suffering?'

We both looked down at the hearthrug, at the place once

occupied by the old dog, and there was silence for several minutes.

Herbert, now seriously ill himself, broke the silence by telling me of the kindness he was now experiencing. A couple he hardly knew came to his home every week and cleaned the house from top to bottom, changing bed linen and cleaning windows. He spoke of the kindness of the community nurse who would go to extraordinary lengths on his behalf, often doing battle with faceless bureaucrats. 'Them's true Christians,' he said, daring me to speak of any other kind!

Sometimes, Herbert thought people were not being kind when they asked him to do something to help himself. Sometimes it is difficult to know what is the kind thing to do. We may not be popular with someone we care for when we encourage them to take pre-scribed exercise or medication, but it would hardly be a kindness to do otherwise. The parent who takes a child to a clinic for a vaccination against a life-threatening illness may cry, along with the child, but will believe, in their heart, that the unpleasant vaccination is necessary and a kindness in the long run.

As I left Herbert that day, he was making his way to the kitchen saying he had been given orders to turn the oven on at a certain time so that it would be ready to receive a meal that would soon arrive. He wasn't best pleased at having to do this little chore, and it would have been easy to do it for him. Whilst I wrestled with the idea of suggesting that I might help, he nudged my elbow and, with a wry smile, said, 'Nurse said I need the exercise.' It can be so easy to misunderstand true kindness.

We discovered, in a previous chapter, a hidden strength in true gentleness. Similarly we may discover something robust in true kindness. When we consider what this virtue reveals to us of God, we might expect it to have something of the quality of good parenting. Much will depend on our experience of human parenting and upon the images of God on which we have been nurtured. Experience of a cruel or overbearing parent may have left us with an image of God that is anything but kind.

When Dorothy, the central character in *The Wizard of Oz*, finally found the Wizard, she and her companions were terrified by his great booming voice that resounded around the Emerald City.

She was both amazed and reassured to find that the Wizard was a kindly old man with a microphone and more than adequate sound amplifiers. Like Dorothy's discovery of the true nature of the Wizard, people discover a God of kindness revealed to us by Jesus Christ.

Nevertheless many people still regard God as fierce and vengeful, breathing fire and punishment. Dorothy found there was more to the kindly old man than she first thought. She discovered the depth of his wisdom and common sense, and through it she and her companions left the Emerald City the richer. In the same way, we meet the kindliness and compassion of God in Jesus but we discover, too, a wise and just God who speaks to us firmly and with authority, bidding us to be brave and courageous, and to cope, with his help, with the difficult decision or the challenging call.

St Paul brought us something of this when he said, 'Note then the kindness and the severity of God.'* His words follow an extended metaphor about the grafting on of branches to a vine. Paul warns the Church in Rome to be on its guard against becoming proud and complacent. He reminds them that they are, by the grace of God, part of his regenerate stock. Paul reserves to God the right to sever faithless branches from the vine, and he balances this with the kindness and mercy of God.

Many Christians find the severity of God reassuring but not always for the best of reasons. There is safety in being exclusive, avoiding meaningful contact with people whose faith in God has been nurtured in other parts of the 'vineyard', and assuming that God will deal severely with those who are 'not quite like us'. When we find God at work in people who are 'not quite like us' in creed, doctrine, authority, or who have little or no formal profession of faith, it challenges the value of what *we* have received. It is like the parable of the labourers in the vineyard.† The system of reward seems to fly in the face of natural justice.

I have very little experience of vineyards, but what I have seen has shown me how widely different they can be. I have seen vineyards in the Greek islands, in Spain, in France and in Italy. They

* Romans 11:22   † Matthew 20:1-16

range from vast flat acres of land with neat rows of vines as far as the eye can see, to little outcrops of vines on steep hillsides where the soil is sparse and the land has been stepped to retain what little rain falls.

After that, the only British vineyard I have visited came as quite a surprise. It was small and neat, and its attractions included a shop selling quite expensive things and a very smart restaurant offering sophisticated food at sophisticated prices. There were gardens to walk round that were neat and tidy, almost twee in parts. There were neat and tidy chickens, and doves in dovecotes. It was very nice indeed but it seemed artificial and contrived compared with those far-off craggy outcrops with vines basking in the sun and longing for moisture.

When Jesus spoke of the kingdom of God being like a vineyard, his followers could look and see what he meant. It was a place of gainful employment, a place of toil and struggle, a place of fruit grown in the most unlikely conditions, an untidy rambling place subject to intruders both animal and human. Imagine someone in this country picking up the Bible in a hotel room and, for want of something else to do, opening at Matthew Chapter 21. Imagine that the reader has only ever seen one vineyard, and it was in Great Britain. He remembered it well; he had a delicious lunch there. It was orderly, tidy, calm and expensive. What, I wonder, might he conclude about the kingdom of God being likened to a vineyard. Compare that man with another reader of the Bible who is black on a white man's estate working for very little money in a vineyard in South Africa. Or perhaps he is the son of the owner of a higgledy-piggledy, barely profitable vineyard somewhere in Croatia. What might they conclude about the kingdom of God?

Isaiah refers to God as the Beloved, the vineyard owner*. The vineyard is not a place but a nation, a nation that God has fashioned himself. God had given his people everything they needed in order to be a people fruitful in their love, devotion and service.

God had set watchtowers in the vineyard (a metaphor for the prophets), to warn and to protect his people. But the people did

* Isaiah 5:1

not grow the fruit of righteousness that God had expected. Now, he is threatening to destroy what he has made. Well, it is his vineyard, this nation of faithless and ungenerous people; he made it and he can destroy it. But in Matthew, the story is rather different. This time the vineyard owner has let the vineyard out to tenants. The tenants are the authorities in Israel. Their crimes against the prophets, including Jesus' own cousin, John the Baptist, are stacked up for judgement. The chief priests and the Pharisees knew Jesus was speaking about them, too. Jesus makes the same dark threats as Isaiah.

The Christian Church has also been likened to a vineyard. We speak of ourselves as labourers in that vineyard. We speak of Christians of other denominations as labouring with us but in another corner of the same vineyard. It is an enduring metaphor. But the warnings are still on the table. If we are to be God's people, and live in the richness of his generous provision, then we must live righteous lives before him. We are not owners but tenants who can be booted out if we do not pull our weight as we labour for the establishment of the kingdom. The fruit we harvest is not brought about by our own labour but by the grace of God: fruit of love, and joy and peace, patience, kindness and goodness, faithfulness, gentleness and self-control. In this regard, the vineyard of the Lord is not a model farm or a private members club where everything is neat and tidy, and only the wealthy can enjoy what is on offer. It is the craggy outcrop of tangled and misshapen vines in need of the gentle rain of compassion and tenderness.

We may visit parts of the Church where vast congregations in serried ranks raise countless hands in the air in praise, just like a vast vineyard on a plain with vines rising toward the sun; but two or three gathered together under a poor vine, in secret or in fear of reprisals, are as much part of the vineyard as any other, bringing forth a crop of righteousness and faithfulness, often alone and unsupported. The tragedy for any church community is that it may have only one experience of 'vineyard', and that is its own, and it will make assumptions about how the vineyard of the Lord should be run.

There is, too, the problem of those who arrive from one part of the Lord's vineyard to another and immediately set about making that part of the vineyard like the one they have left behind, believing their own experience to be the definitive version of vineyard living. They scorn what that community claims as a bumper harvest, because, to them, it is a handful of raisins, nothing more than dried-up old fruit. And judgement sets in. However, they discover, sooner or later, that here the soil is different, the climate different, the terrain is different, expectations are different. What God praises as increase is different.

Both in the Book of Isaiah, and in the Gospel according to Matthew, the vineyard owner is the one who will judge and not the hired help. The fruit he looks for is not the fruit we might think of as valuable. The bumper crop may be sour and useless for wine-making, but the raisin few he ferments into a potent brew using his own recipe for the nourishment of a spiritually hungry world. In this sense, the world is God's vineyard and it is not bounded by the limits of the Church. When we discover true virtue in people with no explicit Christian allegiance, it challenges Christians used to a narrower definition of vineyard. Judgements are made; even blood has been shed. The warning of Jesus that we should not judge others lest we be ourselves judged* is quickly forgotten.

Jesus speaks of the day that the Son of Man comes in judgement.† He speaks of two men working in a field: one will be taken, the other left. Those words of Jesus, recorded by Matthew, are some of the most spine-chillingly awesome words in the Gospels. When they were first heard by friends of Jesus, and his enemies alike, they must have sent a shiver down the spine, the listeners drawing just a little nearer to the camp-fire.

No doubt, over the centuries, preachers have brought to those words many other words of admonition or warning, or words of comfort or encouragement. The questions are these: Do those words of Jesus – strong words about his coming to judge us – have any sort of impact on us at all? And if they don't touch us, move us and draw us nearer to the warmth for comfort, then why don't they?

* Matthew 7:1 † Matthew 24:40

None of us knows the day or the hour of Christ's return, and few of us are moved to great concern about that. Few people are prepared to go out and radically change their lifestyle, their pattern of discipleship or their model of stewardship. It seems that few people live in any fear of a Day of Judgement, a day we are told to expect. Yet people talk fairly easily of judgement when they see misfortune fall upon their neighbour with whom they have had a long-standing border dispute! 'God doesn't pay his debts in money!' is something I have heard said many times. It would seem that even those with no religious allegiance have a theology of judgement!

St Paul wrestles with this very subject of judgement. The argument went around those early Christians, who were convert Jews, that God, in sending Jesus Christ as the long-awaited Messiah, had come to rescue his own chosen people. As chosen of God and precious to him, they must surely be saved. The question of the salvation of the Gentiles, even convert Gentile Christians, was still being discussed around those same firesides.

I don't know any more about olive groves than I know about vineyards but I am told that Paul's words about grafting branches on to olive trees does not bear too much horticultural inspection! He makes the point, though, that the strange grafting together of Jew and Gentile within the one stock produces growth which is nothing short of miraculous. It is miraculous because it has depended entirely on God's grace to make it grow at all. Grafted in as we are, by grace, it is difficult to imagine how we can suffer as a result of God's stern judgement.

But, as members together of the Body of Christ, we are interdependent parts, organs and limbs of the one Body. When one part of the Body hurts, the whole Body is affected. Likewise, when one part of the Body is in serious sin, the whole of the Body is dishonoured. For that we stand together to be judged together.

In asking us to observe the kindness and severity of God, Paul is asking us to consider not only the judgement of God but the mercy of God. Mercy and judgement. Kindness and severity. If we consider the one without the other we do not do justice to God. It is the one held with the other that makes it possible to contemplate everlasting life with God.

Without taking for granted the kindliness of God, we begin to understand that we do not fear judgement because we have taken on board the idea of a merciful God. This is the God who holds on to the possibility of our return as his prodigal children long after mere humans would have given up on us. We have a God whose love will not give up, a God who is prepared to wait for us to see sense and to be drawn to his searching light. It is a light which, ultimately, we cannot resist. It is by this same kindly light that Jesus shows us to the Father.

If we believe in a God of mercy we should show by our words and actions that mercy is the root of our confidence. The kindness and mercy we show become a sign among us of God's proclivity to be kind, to make allowance, to be merciful. By what we say, and by what we do, we can show a God of mercy to a self-doubting generation. This means showing mercy to each other time and time again. We are to be ambassadors of this merciful God, and we have countless opportunities to show mercy to those who wound us, to those who ignore us, and to those who mock or tease us. Let's hope that the Church will be as merciful as God is, and that it will always remember the words of Jesus: 'Blessed are the merciful, for they shall obtain mercy.'* We may then find that true kindness and mercy are one and the same.

* Matthew 5:7

Focus for reflection

Put on, then, garments that suit God's chosen and beloved people: compassion, kindness, humility, gentleness, patience.
Colossians 3:12

Questions for discussion

1. Can you recall an act of kindness that brought God to mind?
2. Have you ever wanted to do an act of kindness but didn't because you were not sure if your motives would be misunderstood?
3. Is it ever kinder to do nothing at all?

Group activity

Perhaps the best acts of kindness are those that no one else knows about. However, within the safety of the group, plan an act of kindness that you will carry out before the group meets again.

Suggestions for prayer

Lord,
where would I be without the kindness of others,
particularly when I have been ill or vulnerable?
Lord, I know that at those times you ministered to me,
bringing new strength and the assurance of your love.
Thank you, Lord.
Amen.

Thank you, Lord,
for those who were kind enough
to encourage me to help myself,
discerning so well when to help
and when to step aside.
Amen.

Teach me, Lord, to be truly kind.
Lord, help me to be merciful to others
even as you are endlessly merciful to me.
Amen.

Chapter Six

Patience

It can be argued that not all patience is virtuous. There is the patience of the thief who waits his moment to target his victim in the street. There is the patience of the aggrieved victim who waits for the opportunity of revenge. On the pavement edges of our cities, prostitutes wait for their next business opportunity. What seems like patience to cursory observation may be something quite different. They may be feeling all sorts of emotions and anxieties: perhaps fearful of challenge by other prostitutes, perhaps terrified of their pimps or of violent clients. Some may be watchful for the police, others may be past caring and their casualness can look like patience. They may be stunned into a half-waking somnambulance by drugs or alcohol that blocks out the pain of what they are experiencing, and their demeanour can look like patience.

It is hard to credit such people with the God-given virtue of patience but it may be more common than we imagine for people trapped in such a world too long, even at a very deep and unconscious level, for escape from their way of life. It may be the hope that the next client will be a knight in shining armour to carry them away on a big white horse. Their longing may simply be for daylight and the few hours' sleep that are a temporary escape into oblivion. At some level there is a God-givenness to their patient waiting and hoping for the best as they endure the worst.

What, then, is *our* experience of the virtue of patience? When I told my parents that I was going to train to be a nurse, they said I didn't have the patience. I never did find out what exactly they meant and I didn't ask at the time because I didn't want to be deterred. Certainly I was not always patient then, and I am not always patient now!

Patience can sometimes be a cover for sloth. Who was it that said it only takes good people to do nothing for evil to prevail?

Sometimes there is a case for doing nothing; indeed, we should do nothing more often than we do. But to do nothing about a situation in which people are oppressed or suffering, where injustice prevails and destroys lives and livelihoods, is neglect.

When a glimmer of the virtue of patience is discerned, there is a glimpse of God. Aspiring to be patient is the beginning of the possibility of greater things. Aspiration for a new and better life is the beginning of repentance and comes from God. In acknowledging this we are to avoid being self-righteous. Jesus warned the self-righteous that tax collectors and prostitutes are entering the kingdom of heaven ahead of them.*

Our patience is tested, particularly, when we are in the company of others. People are thrown together in all sorts of circumstances, and even the casual observer can marvel at how well people tolerate each other, even if it is only for a short period of time! We do accommodate each other rather well, exercising remarkable patience. Recently I travelled on a London underground train in the rush hour. I counted 35 other people in the small space near the doors. We were crammed together so tightly that I thought I would faint. My only concern was that if I fainted I would have nowhere to fall and that would cause panic by increasing the crush. After a few minutes, people began to adjust to their environment, to accommodate each other. They moved a shoulder here and an arm there. They turned a little to avoid the breath of this one and the offending armpit of another. We were no less densely packed but I felt less oppressed. We had adjusted to that which we could not overcome. Becoming irate or aggressive was in no one's interest. This was one instance when, if all were to survive, there was nothing to be gained by selfishness and everything to be gained by patience. If we were stuck in a tunnel, that might be a different matter. Then we might have one pressure too many, and behaviour might change causing panic, mayhem, injury or even death. We all understood the need for tolerance and patience but without a word being said. More recently, some rail travellers, interviewed by the media following horrendously

* Matthew 21:28-31

disrupted journeys, showed remarkable patience and under-standing.

Let us imagine a long queue at the post office. People are waiting patiently for their turn to be served. The counter clerk comes out from behind the glass screen and goes up to a woman waiting near the end of the queue. He says to her, 'That parcel looks heavy and you have been holding it for a long time. Come to the front of the queue and I will serve you next.' Or to another he says, 'You look tired from standing for so long. Come along and let me get you your pension ahead of these others.' Can you imagine the reaction from some of the others in the queue! True patience is so easily tested along with the virtue of generosity. We see how virtues are interlinked. In this example alone we sense how the counter clerk's kindness might be the testing of the virtues of gentleness, goodness and love.

So often patience is linked with waiting. Henri Nouwen describes this so well: 'A waiting person is a patient person. The word "patience" means the willingness to stay where we are and to live the situation out to the full in the belief that something hidden there will manifest itself to us.' He writes, too, of God's endless patience with us; of God who waits for our response to his great love for us.*

When we wait patiently, whether in a queue at the post office or when we wait patiently for important news or a coming celebration, we echo the God who waits patiently for our whole-hearted response to his call. I find the patience and long-suffering of others very humbling, for in wholesome patience I encounter the patient God: the God whose patience I try every day!

One of the most challenging aspects of patience, as a virtue, is only explored when it is turned on its head. Is impatience always lacking in virtue? For example, the prisoner of war waiting patiently for release but who tries to escape has a duty to do so. Is he being impatient? Is the patient toleration of abuse or evil kind to oneself or to the abuser?

As we reflect on the virtue of patience we might discern a kind

* *The Path of Waiting,* Henri J. M. Nouwen (Darton, Longman & Todd)

of virtuous *impatience* that is characteristic of the human condition and found, for instance, in youthful enthusiasm and zest for life. But we might hope that the same virtue will mature into tolerance of others, and that it won't turn into a destructive impatience.

Darren, a university undergraduate, said of himself, 'I have a bad temper and a habit of speaking the truth as I see it. It sometimes gets me into trouble.' There was about that young man the freshness and openness of someone with the world at his feet and with endless horizons to explore. We might even have recognised something of him in ourselves. However, there is the sense that, if he is to reach his full potential, he may have to learn a degree of circumspection. He may not always find it prudent to say what he thinks, or to subject others to his bad temper. Such remarks remind one of a fashion for frankness that seems to turn an aspect of human frailty into a virtue. To speak one's mind, regardless, and to beat people around the head with angry words seems to have become a hallmark of sophisticated contemporary society.

We like to think of ourselves as civilised people, and yet all of us are aware of the degree of violence in our society. Fuelled by anger and intolerance, it ranges from bullying in the school playground and in the workplace, to road rage, and to covert violence within families. It ranges from the serious street violence that accompanies organised crime, to the fight between two octogenarians over a packet of custard creams on the bargain counter at the local supermarket. It would seem that people have changed very little over the centuries. Then, as now, we can still regard such aggressive impatience as a failure to live up to the ordinances of God. Among the less familiar writings of the ancient world is the Book of Ecclesiasticus in the Apocrypha, written by a man called Sirach. He had observations to make about human behaviour that have a contemporary resonance to them.

Sirach – properly called Jesus, Son of Eleazor, Son of Sira – was an educated and cultured man who was born and bred in Jerusalem some two hundred years before Christ. After long service in the diplomatic corps he ran a school and wrote his book as a guideline for those who wished, sincerely, to keep the commandments of God. The early Church valued his book as a sort of guideline for Christian behaviour, and much of its wisdom is relevant today, not least a section on anger and rage.* The wisdom of young Darren is answered by the wisdom of Sirach who advises us to avoid quarrels kindled by a hot temper. He goes on to say 'the more fuel, the fiercer the blaze, the more stubborn the defence, the fiercer the fight.'†

From this scrap of scripture, it was verse 5 that caught my attention in particular. Sirach asks, 'If a mere mortal cherishes rage, where is he to look for pardon?" Here we begin to see the difference between rage which is an unhappy and regrettable show of our baser nature, and rage which is cherished, held dear, maintained and protected.

Now we begin to see the difference between getting angry – losing our temper – and developing a mindset of anger that passes for a virtue of honesty – saying it like it is. There is something human and understandable about rage as a spontaneous reaction to great provocation. Even the law courts recognise the difference between spontaneous provoked rage and premeditated violent crime.

It is when the balance shifts from rage as a regrettable manifestation of human weakness to rage as the engine of an armoured truck that flattens all before it in single-minded determination to get where one wants to go, that sight is lost of a God who calls us to account for our behaviour.

Moving forward in history by a couple of hundred years and into the early Christian era, we find that St John, the writer of the Book of Revelation, is himself enraged by the way the Roman Empire is treating the Christian Church. In his powerful vision of God's judgement, the Christians on earth look to God for vindication.‡ Their prayers are brought before the throne of God by an angel, his smoking censor symbolising the earnest prayers of God's people. In a dramatic gesture, the angel throws the censor, sending it crashing down to the earth. It is a violent act born out of John's rage on behalf of the persecuted Church. We might ask

* Ecclesiasticus 27:30-28:12   † Ecclesiasticus 28:10   ‡ Revelation 8:3-5

ourselves where that leaves us. John is standing to one side of us holding one end of a tightrope, and Sirach is standing to the other side, with the other end. We are asked to balance on a tightrope somewhere between justifiable anger and the cherishing of rage. We learn to walk the tightrope as we go through life. Let's hope that Darren learns that too!

We encounter natural and understandable anger that is part of the expression of the pain of grief. Sometimes it is only anger that can get an injured man up off the ground to safety and help. It has been rage against injustice that has brought many brave people in South America to champion the poor and the persecuted. It has been rage that has rescued children from exploitation in the sweatshops of the Far East.

All too often the response to people's justifiable rage has been mind-controlling indoctrination, or drug-induced blandness and pseudo-tranquillity, that has made slaves of people, their personalities flattened beyond recognition. To our shame, this form of abuse has sometimes been carried out in the name of the living God. Many would say that a little more rage in the Church would do more for the kingdom than the more corrosive and pervasive apathy.

There is a balance to be maintained somewhere between the extremes of self-controlled humanity flattened by the internalisation of natural emotion on the one hand, and humanity that makes a virtue of violent self-expression on the other. There are, too, for each of us moments of choice: opportunities to choose a response to provocation that is honest and expresses the strength of our feeling, but a response which does not brow-beat, bully or depersonalise another whose view of life is different from our own. Moments of choice may be milliseconds long, but they can be cultivated.

If we develop an attitude which views others as being precious in the eyes of God, we learn to come before them like Moses came before God in the burning bush. 'Take off your shoes,' said the Lord, 'for the place where you are standing is holy ground.' In the millisecond we have before we respond to others, there is just time for the entrance into our consciousness of the value, preciousness and nobility, in the sight of God, of the person before us. This millisecond of choice is the school of patience. Not unlike the device of counting up to ten before responding impatiently. Long enough to send up a prayer: 'God give me patience!'

On a lifelong pilgrimage the Christian tightrope walker meets the living, loving and compassionate Lord who teaches us how to channel our God-given and strong emotions into table-overturning championship of the poor and downtrodden, but who gently and firmly teaches us to recognise holy ground when we meet it in others, and who prompts us, by his Spirit, to make appropriate behavioural choices.

Whilst making allowances for the youthful Darrens of this world, with their sparkle and energy that 'says it like it is', we learn to marvel at the patience shown by many people in the most trying of situations. In both we see something of the God who lovingly and patiently shapes and crafts the full range of human emotion into something glorious for him.

Focus for reflection

You must be patient, my friends, until the Lord comes.
James 5:7

Questions for discussion

1. Do you have a short fuse? If so, can you do anything about it?
2. What situations try your patience most?
3. Do you get impatient with yourself?

Group activity

• Is there a hobby activity that you have thrown to the back of a cupboard because you were frustrated with it? Could you find it again, and have one more go at completing it or at least moving the project on beyond the difficulty? Bring it to the group meeting, next time, and see if anyone else can help to sort it out.

• Make a resolution to be more patient with a particular person, or to wait more patiently in queues or to be served in a restaurant or shop. Work out a 'mantra' or other device for filling the waiting time with a sense of God's patient presence.

Suggestions for prayer

Lord,
I am not the most patient of people;
sometimes frustration or irritation gets the better of me.
Help me to hear your gentle chiding,
your calm voice bidding me to be patient.
Help me to breathe deeply of your patient Presence,
so that I may respond more often
in a way that does you honour.
Amen.

Sometimes, Lord,
I think enthusiasm and zeal for your kingdom
gives me permission to be impatient with people.
Teach me your ways,
and guide me so that I help build *your* kingdom
and not a monument to my own ego.
Amen.

Be always patient, Lord, with your people,
and teach us to wait upon you.
Amen.

Chapter Seven

Peace

Claire had collected all the candles in the house and had lit them in the bathroom. She locked the door before sinking into the fragrant foam-filled bath. She sighed deeply. Aloud she exclaimed, 'Peace at last!' It was a prayer but she barely knew it. It was a prayer of thanksgiving for a blessed respite from the problems that threatened to overwhelm her. It was the recognition of a moment, an interlude of peace.

But was it a true peace that Claire experienced? It would not last because even as she lay in the bath she picked up and examined, in her mind, each of her problems as if she were browsing in an antique shop. All her problems would be there when she emerged from the bathroom but, for now, even though she considered them, she did so in an abstract sort of a way. For the moment she had respite from them. The foamy water covered her and protected her from the impact of them. It was a God-given moment, a pledge of peace.

For it to be true and lasting peace it would have to embrace the tensions and paradox of our life. Setting aside the stresses in our life may bring brief respite, but it is an unreal peace. A truer peace is that which can embrace the tensions within us – love and hate, joy and sadness, listlessness and drivenness.

Claire had briefly distanced herself from her problems. Aloud to the bathroom wall she was not going to worry about anything. For now, she was able to address the patterns on the wall tiles, rehearsing to them her feelings and saying to the wall that she was past caring about everything. But of course she wasn't really. She was wise enough to know that she was simply taking time out to renew her energies, the better to cope with the problems that beset her. Being 'past caring' what happens to us – being without energy, without hope or passion – is no peace at all: merely an escape from the prison of life's trials. Claire didn't necessarily want escape from her troubles. She would settle for parole. More lasting peace for Claire would come not from the end of her problems nor in finding solutions for them, but in reaching an understanding of the nature of them; in discerning the difference between the problems that are resolvable and those that are to be accommodated until they can be resolved.

Had she known it, Claire might have liked that prayer attributed to Reinhold Niebuhr: 'God grant me the serenity to accept the things I cannot change; the courage to change the things I can; and the wisdom to know the difference.' To use again the analogy of browsing in an antique shop, Claire would consider the provenance of a problem: where it came from, what its significance might be as well as its value. Trying to learn the difference is another way of saying that we need to learn to differentiate between the ills of society that are beyond our power to change and the ones that we might just be able to influence a tiny bit. It seems to take some of us a lifetime to begin to discern the difference. Meanwhile, 'serenity' – a kind of peace – comes over us like warm fragrant water, in brief and precious moments. We will return to Claire later in the chapter. For now, she is safe behind a locked door!

Let us consider now the relationship between peace and passion. People can feel so passionate about something that they cannot rest until they have achieved their objective, reached their goal, or solved their problem. Yet they can be at peace knowing deep down that their goal, objective or passion is right, just and true. This to be distinguished from obsession and drivenness which is a kind of madness and is destructive. Being disturbed and fired-up in our spirit brings its own peace.

I recall a very elderly person who rarely leaves her home, but who is also one of the best-informed people I know. Through television and radio, she keeps herself abreast of world news, and each time I call she quizzes me on some of the news items that have made an impression on her. Inevitably, the news being what it is, she recalls accounts of violent crime, of scandalous affairs, of tragedies and disasters, both man-made and natural. Mostly, her close questioning of me is based on just one question: 'What do you think the world is coming to?' I *want* to reply that the world is coming to the feet of the Lord in repentance and obedience. I want to say that, but I don't know if it is true. I believe in the ultimate victory of God over sin and death. I believe, too, that God is in the world reconciling it to himself. There are many different views on how the world will end. One view is that there will be disaster and destruction on a global scale, brought on by ourselves; another is a vision of the calming of the seas, the silencing of the volcanoes, the harnessing of destructive wind, and humankind consecrated, transformed and enveloped in the Love of God. 'What is the world coming to?' I have no answer for her. To be fair, I am not sure she expects me to have one. We may ask ourselves, 'Is the world moving towards total annihilation or total consecration?' We may not have an answer to that question either. What we do know is that when we see violent crime portrayed so graphically on television, or when two people, before our very eyes, tear each other apart, physically or verbally, then we know how much savage there is, still, in all of us.

We might suppose from all we see and hear and read in the media that there is little hope for humankind. Stories of love, peace and compassion rarely hit the headlines: they don't sell newspapers, and they don't sell airtime. But we sense and experience super-human heroism. We see and experience, in our own lives and in the accounts of others, the very best that human nature is capable of, and, as Christians, we understand such phenomena as being evidence of the presence of the transforming grace of God.

'What is the world coming to?' The answer may be up to us all, and how far we have evolved; how successfully we can make the transition from savagery to civilisation, and embrace the law of love given to us by Jesus. Henri Nouwen suggests that waiting is not entirely passive; that when we wait patiently we move from something to something more.*

He also suggests that one reason why people find waiting so difficult is fear. Many people today are afraid of their inner feelings, of their present circumstances, or they may be afraid of what others might do to them. We may be afraid to do nothing and have a

* *The Path of Waiting,* Henri J. M. Nouwen (Darton, Longman & Todd)

distorted idea of the imperative to do something. We may say to ourselves, 'Surely, I must do *something*. I cannot sit and do nothing.' Then again, we may do nothing for fear of doing the wrong thing, and this sets up a tension within us. Should we fight, react, resist? Should we sit tight and wait to see what happens; endure, tolerate, accept? We may find ourselves locked into this loop of life-draining anxiety, with no sense of how to escape from it.

Let us return to Claire in her locked bathroom. She might be ready to emerge from her foam-filled haven.

Her door is still locked against the world. It might bring to mind another locked door on another occasion long ago. It is the story of how the disciples of Jesus, following his death, were hiding in fear behind locked doors.*

It was still Sunday, the Day of Resurrection, only the fourth day since the arrest of Jesus in the Garden of Gethsemane. The eleven disciples had fled in terror and, presumably, hidden themselves away behind locked doors for fear of capture, and, seeing the fate of Jesus, for fear that they themselves might be taken, tortured and killed. There was a very real threat to their life. It is easy to be disdainful of them but really they were being prudent. They needed space and time to think what to do. With Jesus gone, the Shepherd was struck and they were like sheep: lost and bewildered; fearful, yes, but with sufficient sense of self-preservation to find each other, and to find a secret and safe place, and to lock themselves away, buying themselves some time to plan, to recover, to build each other up.

Although most of us may not have experienced such dire circumstances, we can empathise with the need, sometimes, for a chance to hide away from the pressures of life, to find space for reflection, rest and healing, for safe companionship; to find a door with a lock on it, and to turn the key against the onslaughts of the world. 'Go away, world, and leave me in peace,' we might say.

I have done a number of parish visits on the doorstep. On one occasion, there was snow on the ground and I had called on someone because I had heard that a grandchild had died. I was

* John 20:19, 26

kept on the doorstep. Eventually, I said, 'Don't let all the heat out of your room, Mrs –.' 'Thank you,' she said, 'I won't,' and promptly closed the door on me! There are quite a few folk who spend months of the year, especially the winter months, behind locked doors, afraid of con men, burglars or adverse weather conditions.

In the Gospel we read that Jesus entered the room where the disciples hid for fear of their enemies, even though the door was locked. We sense the power of the Resurrection as the Lord cuts through the laws of nature, through solid wood doors. He had gone through so much for his disciples, and now he goes further in order to bring them peace at a very difficult time for them.

But one of them, Thomas, was missing. He was not there to hear the words, 'Peace be with you.' He was not there to know the reassuring presence of the risen Lord, to feel his touch on shaking hands, his calming breath on anxious faces.

Thomas's assertion that he would not believe unless he had proof may have been more about pique than doubt. There they were, the other ten disciples, looking like the cat that had got the cream. They had seen the Lord, they had known his reassuring touch, and heard his blessing of peace. Disappointed, hyper-sensitive because of the stress of the situation – put out, to say the least – Thomas needed what they had been given. Once again, Jesus, set free by his resurrection to go anywhere and do any-thing in power, returns to the room for Thomas's sake.

It has often been said that, when it comes to St John's Gospel, it is the little things that matter. It is the odd word or phrase that is loaded with meaning and significance. St John has to be read carefully, word by word: savoured and reflected upon if the voice of the Spirit of God is going to be heard in our hearts. This time, the significance might be found in the way the locking of the doors is described, first in verse 19 and then in verse 26. In the New Revised Standard Version we are told that on the second occasion the doors were shut. Not locked but shut. Locked on the first occasion but shut on the second. Could it be that John wants us to understand that, in the week that has passed, the disciples have become a little braver, a little less anxious; that the peace of Christ has begun to rule in their hearts? I do hope so, because what it says to us is that the words of Jesus are more than pious platitudes.

The words of Jesus have authority over our racing pulses, over our rapid and shallow breathing, over anxious minds filled with dread. Enough at least to allow the disciples to leave the door shut but unlocked. Jesus had begun to work on human hearts from beyond the cross and the sepulchre, and look what trouble he goes to in order to bring about even the tiniest difference: the turning of a key in a lock! The choice of the translator, on this occasion, brings such hope and promise, but dare we hope that this translation will stand up to academic scrutiny? A comparison of the words used in verses 19 and 26 in the original Greek does not support the theory of a difference between the two occasions, but the wording in the Latin Vulgate does. In that translation Jerome used the phrase *fores eesent clausae* – 'when the doors had been shut'. In verse 26 he uses the phrase *ianuis clausis* – 'the doors having been shut'. The clue lies not in the construction but in the use of a different word for door: on the first occasion *fores* which was more of an outer door, like the door to a compound or yard; on the second occasion the word *ianuis* refers to a house door. We can presume that shut means barred in some way and therefore effectively locked on both occasions, but, whereas on the first occasion no one was allowed through either the outer barrier or the inner barrier, on the second occasion the inner barrier was all that stood between the disciples and the world they feared.

It may be that Jerome had access to, and had been influenced by, a Greek manuscript that is now lost to us. It may be that he was giving this scripture a personal theological interpretation, supporting the idea of there being a gradual opening up, an 'unlocking' of the disciples' fear and the first signs of a growing confidence.

Their confidence would grow and grow as Jesus continued to minister to them. He would breathe on them all, and give them the Holy Spirit. He would teach and train them, appearing whenever they had a spiritual or material need. He would encourage and empower them. In a few short weeks their lives would be turned upside down, and they would be showered with the gifts his Spirit would bring. Soon enough, this tiny band of fearful disciples would be bold and courageous Apostles, sent out to the whole world to proclaim the Good News.

But it starts with the soft turning of a key – not yet brave but prepared to try and be brave. Not yet bold and outspoken but less afraid of being violently silenced. And the initiative and the effort? Entirely that of Jesus.

The lesson for us seems to be that God can change lives for the better. But the significance of the locked door is that Jesus will not be kept out or at arm's length. He can and does break through the spiritual and temporal barriers we put up: the excuses we make, the demands we make for proof.

His initiative is both gentle and strong. Nothing will prevent him from bringing peace where peace is required, but we may say that there is still a yawning gap between the ideal of peace and our experience of it.

In almost every act of worship on every Sunday of the year we pray for peace. Our prayers for peace are heightened, intensified, in the face of a new conflict, a new atrocity, a new violation of a peace agreement.

People have always turned to their God to ask him to make peace among his people. Sceptics might have grounds for saying, 'Since you have asked your God time and time again for peace, why is there still war? Is your God not interested? Is he there at all?'

The scriptures are clear: peace is a gift from God. Jesus himself breathed on his disciples and gave them a gift of peace, but their lives were not peaceful. There were battles to fight: spiritual, intellectual and physical. They overcame both man-made and natural disasters, and they all met violent deaths at the hands of their enemies. The peace Jesus gave was about a relationship with God and not about feeling peaceful.

When we ask God for his gift of peace we must be clear about what we expect of him, and what we don't. This seems far from easy. We don't, for instance, expect peace to descend on us in a cloud of tranquillisers producing in us a zombie-like peace, a kind of 'spaced out' peace that is no peace at all.

St Paul described peace as 'fruit' of the Spirit: the harvest, the outcome of obedience to God and his commandments, especially his commandment that we love one another. Peace, then, is both the grace of God's gifting and the product of the effort people put in to achieving it.

Sometimes it seems that we pray for peace hoping that God will descend from heaven and intervene, like the teacher who comes between two children fighting in the playground, sorts them out, gets to the bottom of the problem before giving them a lecture. Then the teacher sends them off with a warning not to get into trouble again. This seemed to be the theology of some children who composed this prayer: 'Dear God, there are many awful things going on in the world. People are killing each other; people are sick and injured and they will die if you don't do something about it. We cannot do anything but you can. Please, God, do something. Amen.'

God has given us so many gifts: generosity, patience, kindness and, supremely, self-sacrificing love. He has given us skills of diplomacy and communication that leave no excuse for misunderstanding. We know how to make the tools and weapons of war, but we have been given the tools for peace if only we could access them and learn how to use them. We may feel we have no influence over peace between nations, but we may be able to make a small difference to peace within our own communities and families, and contribute through the democratic processes to the decisions being made at national and international levels.

As we have discovered in earlier chapters, virtue is a revelation of God and where there is a revelation of God, there is his kingdom. This hypothesis stands in relation to peace. 'We have peace with God the Father through our Lord Jesus Christ'.* People of peace manifest the God of peace, and that peace is robust and full of passion. It fires us up to work for justice and peace. It is seated deep in our will. It is for this reason that humankind demands more of peace than the cessation of hostility, though many would be glad of that.

Now we come closer to an understanding of the meaning of true peace. True peace is that which Jesus came to bring – namely

* Romans 5:1

reconciliation between us and his Father, an end to the cold war of sin and disobedience. In this we have peace with God through Jesus Christ. It is a peace that is seated deep in our will and has little to do with our emotions. In God-given moments of relative peace we may glimpse 'the peace which passes all understanding'.* Essentially, it is a peace rooted in the God of Peace.

* Philippians 4:7

Focus for reflection

Peace is my parting gift to you, my own peace, such as the world cannot give.
John 14:27

Questions for discussion

1. If we pray for peace, why is there not peace in the world?
2. Are you at peace with all the people you know? If not, is there something you can do to make peace with them?
3. Are you at peace with God?

Group activity

Spend some time quietly together. Think about the symbols and emblems that are used to represent 'peace' before doodling with crayons and paper to create your own symbol. Share your design and its meaning with a partner or with the rest of the group.

Activity for one!

Resolve to find for yourself 'time out' from the stresses and problems that beset you. Decide how you will spend the time and where you will spend it. If you are going to lock the door to your space, you may need to explain this to others! Perhaps music, pleasant aromas or soft lighting might help. Before emerging from your 'time out', resolve to recall the presence of the God of peace as you return to your daily pursuits.

Suggestions for prayer

Lord,
help me to remember
that just because I do not feel peaceful,
it does not mean I am not at peace
with you or with others.
Help me to see that sometimes
my impatience is really zeal for your kingdom.
Amen.

Lord,
help all your people to be peacemakers,
but especially bless those to whom you have given gifts
for negotiation and reconciliation.
Help all who work so hard for peace between nations,
peace within communities,
peace among family members.
Amen.

Lord,
bring your healing peace
to all who are anxious or distressed,
and bless, too, those who care for them
and who may not know what to say or do to help.
Amen.

Chapter Eight

Joy

We now approach the summit of the mountain of virtue. Through the foothills of self-control, gentleness and faithfulness we discovered the God of Presence who warms us into a relationship with him that melts our obsession with being in control without losing sight of the need for discipline. God, who has taken the initiative in keeping faith with us, helps us to find the courage and strength to be gentle with ourselves and with others. We have found the faithful God who calls us to show his faithfulness to a faltering world. We move through the basics of decent human behaviour and begin to climb through virtues of goodness, kindness and patience. We discover a holy God in ourselves and in others. We find there, too, a robust kindness in God and dynamic patience that draws and energises us, and engenders in us a zeal to be more like him. This good, faithful and merciful God has wrapped us gently but firmly in his compassion and brought us true peace, without an expectation that we will feel peaceful. With each step and turn of our holy pilgrimage we recognise God in the fruit of his Spirit; we glimpse the summit of the God of Love, and joy fills our heart. Here we pause to reflect on joy and its place in the Christian life and tradition.

First, we explore the meaning of joy. We begin our search in the scriptures where the word 'joy' is used both as a noun and as a verb: the verb 'to joy' as in 'to be glad'. Verbs, I seem to recall from school days, are doing words and suggest effort. To be glad – to joy in a situation – requires an act of will rather than an emotional response. 'To joy' is to get up and do something, rather than hope that joy will overcome us, unexpectedly. In Psalm 21, for instance, we read, 'The King shall joy in your strength, O Lord',* translated sometimes as 'In your strength the king rejoices, O Lord'.†

To joy is to rejoice. To feel that we can rejoice, we might say we need a trigger of some kind. From where will this rejoicing well up

---

* Authorised Version   † Revised Standard Version

inside us? Is it, perhaps, from gratitude? Is it from awe or wonder, as with the joy that a new baby brings? So often, joy is brought to us by 'joy-bearers', like the angels that brought joy to the shepherds on the hillsides of Bethlehem. They came with the joyful news of the birth of Jesus.

On that occasion 'joy' was given greater meaning: 'Behold! I bring you good news of a great joy which will come to all the people.'* Great joy – joy as a noun; as a fact. The significance of the coming of the Christ child was yet to be understood by the shepherds or by anyone else. The details of the story are never far from us. The shepherds went and found the child Jesus and afterwards went on their way rejoicing and glorifying God.† Something of the joyousness of the occasion had touched them. They had been touched by joy as if it were a tangible thing. It was a life-changing encounter for them.

We might pause on our journey to reflect on who have been the 'joy-bearers' in our own life. We may consider that we have never had such a spectacular and life-changing experience, but we may recognise occasions, moments even, when meeting some-one has changed our life for the better. It may have been only a fleeting relationship but it left us with a new insight into God, our-selves or the world around us. It could have been as casual as a remark made by a stranger on a station platform, someone who came fleetingly into our life and had a kind of message to deliver. It was as if they had read our mind and sensed our mood, and their remark changed how we perceived a problem, or spurred us into some action that opened up opportunities for personal growth. They brought a kind of joy, perhaps not the somersault-turning kind of joy, but the deep sense of well-being and arrival that made us believe that their appearance had something to do with God. Then they were gone. Later, when we wanted to say, 'Thank you' or 'Tell me more' they were not to be found. It was as if they had been angels. Whoever they were, they made joy present; they made God present.

Essentially, such experiences are the same as that of the

* Luke 2:10   † Luke 2:20

shepherds of Bethlehem, but perhaps our twenty-first-century minds have difficulty with such a notion. We might have come to think of angels (if we think of them at all) as heavenly beings sitting on clouds and plucking at harps!

The angels we encounter in the Bible seem to be messengers (the Greek word for angel is *angelos* and also means messenger) but they are more than that. To encounter an angel is to encounter an anthropomorphism of God himself.

Take, for example, the story of Abraham and the three visitors under the oak tree at Mamre.* Abraham entertains three strangers – angels – but the text clearly indicates that Abraham met the Lord himself. Christian tradition, especially in the Eastern Church, has long held that these three visitors were a manifestation of God in Trinity: Father, Son and Holy Spirit.

In this way an angel is said to make God present; what an angel brings, in terms of words or gifts, is of God himself. For instance, the overshadowing of the Virgin Mary, which resulted in her mystical pregnancy, was brought by the Archangel Gabriel, making both God the Holy Spirit and his actions a present, divine and human reality. The process, then, is one of God making himself, and therefore his characteristics, present and in many ways. The scriptures call some of those ways the ministry of angels who bring something of God to humanity. Angels are the God of Joy made present.

In this way, joy as noun, as an attribute of God and as a sign of God's presence, is manifest to us in angelic encounters that bring great joy, and which are instilled in our hearts to be manifest again in the experience of being joyed, of rejoicing.

So far, then, we have considered joy as an attribute – a characteristic of God – and as noun – as the God of Joy. We might say that where we find God, we find joy, but I assert that where we find joy, we find God! To find him, our senses need to be open to how he might make his presence known.

I think of the weeks before Christmas. For Christians it is the lovely season of Advent. It is the sense-sharpening season: a time to allow ourselves the possibility of the mystical and spiritual as a

* Genesis 18

dimension to our human and eternal existence. In Advent we keep one eye on the heavens above for the powerful presence of God and of the angelic host, and one ear open to the sound of the voice of our returning Saviour. It is a season both of joy and of anticipatory joy.

Training our senses to be open to God is part of the discipline of prayer and of Christian living. It is vital in all seasons of the year, but in Advent we learn a bit more about how to be open to God's tuition. We learn how to let the awe and the wonder of God pervade and overwhelm us.

Sometimes life events or circumstances have a similar effect on us. Times of great stress or anxiety can be times when our senses are heightened. Bereavement is one such time. We can be hyper-sensitive to a clumsy word from a friend, or easily moved to tears in the most unlikely situations or circumstances. New senses are awakened, perspectives changed, perceptions changed. Out of the darkness and the pain of grief can come incredible personal growth, not only emotional growth, but spiritual growth too. Later, we may see this as the hand of God. Out of death and loss comes the resurrection experience. We begin to see the possibility of the text from the Book of Revelation: 'Behold I make all things new.'*

We may know people who have emerged from the devastation of bereavement, redundancy, divorce or a broken love affair with new and amazing spiritual insights. On the way, they have recognised that their senses were heightened; they were looking and listening for signs – signs of God's love and mercy, signs of hope; signs of a promise of reunion with their loved ones. They have known deep spiritual yearnings, mixed with hope, anticipation, and, yes, sometimes, and to their great surprise, even joy. For many, the worst of their grief was something of an Advent. The colour was purple: the reflection deep, but the openness to the signs was great indeed.

Identifying joy in ourselves or in others can be quite difficult. To do so we might find it helpful to distinguish between 'joy' and

* Revelation 21:5

'happiness'. I suggest that happiness is experienced at an emotional level, and is transient, temporary and dies with us, whereas joy is experienced at a deeper level, at the level of the will and lasts for ever in the God of Joy. In this sense, one could say that a close personal relationship may be characterised by a deep and inter-connected joy which is constant: down there in the gut, too deep to express in words, and beyond emotional lability. To use another analogy, happiness is to affection what joy is to love. We may ask ourselves, or each other, if we are happy, and the answer may depend upon the day of the week or the mood of the moment. The more pertinent question would be: Is there deep and lasting joy in this relationship that transcends the emotional 'big dipper'? Joy resides in a part of us that is too deep in the ocean of our being to be seriously disturbed by surface and superficial happiness/unhappiness emotions.

Before leaving happiness too far out in the cold, we might reflect on true and false happiness. Once again, the scriptural use of the word may help us. In the scriptures, happiness is closely related to 'blessedness'. For example, in some translations of the opening verses of the fifth chapter of St Matthew Gospel we find the word 'happy' used for that of 'blessed' as in 'Happy are the poor in spirit, for the kingdom of heaven is theirs.'*

Where this translation of blessed (*makarios*) clashes horribly with the modern use of the word happy is in verse 4 of the same chapter: 'Happy are those who mourn; God will comfort them!' Not something to say to the recently bereaved. 'Blessed are those who mourn', favoured by most biblical scholars, brings with it a sense of the protectiveness, the caring, the redeeming nature of God. The emphasis is on the reaching-out of a benevolent God rather than on our own search for a feeling of well-being that we may not find, at least not at that time.

A browse through the Old Testament may give us some clues as to why it can be difficult to distinguish between 'blessedness' and 'happiness'. There we discover a belief among God's people that a man was said to be blessed by God if he had a good wife,

* Matthew 5:3, Good News Bible

lots of children (preferably sons), crops in the field and goods in store. Conversely, if there was famine, his children died of fever or robbers emptied his store, he might think of himself as cursed by God. Wealth, affluence, position, prestige were signs of being blessed and spawned a view of happiness with the devastating corollary that without wealth, affluence, position or prestige, there could be only unhappiness. With the passing of years, decades and millennia, the pursuit of happiness, for some, has become synonymous with the pursuit of worldly gain. Threads of our distant past seem to hold us down like those that attempted to restrain Gulliver in Lilliput.

There is, of course, a feeling, an emotion of happiness, that is part and parcel of wholesome human life. Certainly, none of us would want to see people unhappy; but if the pursuit of happiness becomes all-consuming, we may be in danger of missing out on joy on the way. In the scriptural translations where the word *makarios* is translated as happy rather than blessed, a footnote is necessary to qualify the meaning as being *true* happiness, as distinct from the kind of false happiness to which many of us cling.

Some parents and some teachers complain that the current generation of youngsters need entertaining much more than the previous generation did. Happiness, it seems, must be provided along with everything else. Happiness, for many, does not come naturally or often, and is much more difficult to find when the mountain of virtue is shrouded in a fog of selfishness. If people cannot show to themselves, or to others, some of the virtues we have been contemplating, how can they reveal God to each other?

Many people try to plug the dark holes in their lives – the voids, the yawning chasms in which they cry noiselessly – with a substitute happiness. They sometimes cry so noiselessly that they do not even draw attention to themselves by their cries. They may plug the holes with addictive substances, so that spiritual pain is dulled, reality is suspended, and fantasy havens offer comparative safety.

I mentioned earlier the lovely season of Advent in which our spiritual senses are on the alert for signs of God's presence. In those same weeks before Christmas, even as the Church and the world anticipate the joy of the Christmas season, many people are caught up in the annual trade fair for fillers of black holes, and the more sophisticated society becomes, the greater the range of hole-fillers is on sale! Even the act of purchasing becomes, for some, a therapy, an addiction. The sign on the highway of life says, 'Beware of substitutes for joy': they are many, and not all are unpleasant, or even unwholesome. Designer goods are easily faked, and for many the fake is good enough and affordable, but when the real thing is available, touched and handled, the difference can be appreciated.

Joy, blessedness, happiness and their corollaries are the warp and weft of life. They get mixed up together in a heady cocktail of human experience. When we are privileged to hear someone's story and to help them to find meaning in all that has happened to them, we merely sit as if side by side on a wayside bench contemplating the view. One such person with whom I once sat was Janet.

Janet's husband had died suddenly and, over the following months, she tried to make sense of all that had happened to her. Her husband had not been a believer and, although she had always had a faith, she had not been a regular church-goer. In her grief, her senses were heightened as she strained for signs of God's abiding love and mercy. She needed reassurance of the well-being of her much-loved husband. She knew enough about Christian teaching to know that the dark arts of psychics and mediums were contrary to biblical teaching and dangerous to her spiritual welfare. She did not look there for a much-needed sign. She prayed for a sign from God that her husband was safe with him.

Outside the sitting room window of their home, there was a fig tree. It had never really borne any fruit. Every year it would produce one fig. Her husband would pick it, bring it into the house, cut it in half, and they would eat it together. It became, to them both, a symbol of the love they shared.

The summer after his death, the fig tree was heavy with figs. It was bowed down with figs. In the breeze they knocked against the glass of the patio doors. Janet took that fruiting as the sign she sought. It was as if God was saying, 'Look at the fig tree, the sign of the love you shared: my love for you both is big enough to overcome all things, even death and disbelief.'

Janet went on to grow in faith, confidence and joy. She has retained her sense of the presence and joy of God. Of course, she still misses her husband terribly. The season is still purple and she is still in the Advent of hopeful anticipation as she waits for the time when the Lord will unite her with her beloved husband.

In summary, joy in scripture and in Christian tradition is a characteristic of God made manifest in humanity. It is deeper than an emotion but can be the wellspring of emotions. True happiness is rooted in the knowledge that one is blest, loved and cared for by God, even in the most adverse of situations. Joy is distinct from happiness but they are close cousins: the Greek word *cara* can be used for either, depending on the context. The relationship between joy and true happiness – blessedness – calls for a distinction between that and false happiness.

Joy, rooted in the will, as a verb or as a noun, implies a dynamic, active and interactive process that may require our effort or co-operation if it is to be developed in us, and a determination to break free from those Lilliputian restraints and so discover true joy in our lives and in the lives of those around us. We need to learn, too, how to 'infect' others with joy in a way that respects that the God of virtue is as present in them as it is in us. We stand before others in whom God dwells, and, like Moses, take off our shoes for we stand on holy ground.* Remembering to take off our shoes in respect will prevent us from being smug, glib or patronising towards those for whom joy is hidden in mountain-top fog. St Paul reminds us that all our efforts are worth nothing without love.[†] The summit of virtue is in sight!

* Exodus 3:5   † 1 Corinthians 13

Focus for reflection

And may God, who is the ground of hope, fill you with all joy and peace as you lead the life of faith until, by the power of the Holy Spirit, you overflow with hope.
Romans 15:13

Questions for discussion

1. Do you believe in angels?
2. Have you been ministered to by angels?
3. Has true joy got anything to do with happiness?
4. Are you ever tempted to think that misfortune is a sign of being out of favour with God?

Group activity

Draw a picture of an angel. As in the iconographical tradition, you might portray your angel as carrying something that has special significance. You may like to share the meaning with others. The group may like to cut out and paste together a montage – a 'myriad' of angels!

Suggestions for prayer

Lord,
I do not always feel joyful –
sometimes far from it!
Be Joy in me and lift my heart in praise.
Help me to remember that I worship
with the whole company of heaven.
Amen.

God's Good Fruit

Lord,
help those who seek true happiness
in things that do not satisfy.
Turn the hearts of those who exploit the joyless
by offering them a 'pseudo' happiness.
Amen.

Help me, Lord,
to rediscover childlike joy in little things,
and in that rediscovery to find you,
the God of all joy.
Amen.

Chapter Nine

Love

Mae West, the famous and rather outrageous entertainer, was often asked about the men in her life. Allegedly, she once replied, 'What counts is not the men in my life, but the life in my men!' I am inclined to borrow from Mae West and to suggest that what counts is not the love in our life, but the life in our love. Notice I didn't say 'loving' for I would like to reflect initially on love as a noun, and further on Love as a proper noun.

Some people I know are appalled and disgusted by the liberal use of the word *love* in modern life. They lament that there is only one word in English for love. The Greek language has at least three: *eros*, the love that a couple shares: *philos*, a kind of fraternal or sororal love, and *agape* which is undersold if we say that it is only about love between God and us.

For a long time, I liked the idea of there being different words to distinguish kinds of love but now I am much more comfortable with the one word because it stops me from trying to pigeon-hole the love I experience in my own life, and in the lives of those around me.

Thinking of myself as the only heretic on the planet I was comforted to read *Love* by Ernesto Cardenal, a disciple of the well-known spiritual writer Thomas Merton, and a member of a contemplative Christian commune in Nicaragua. His work reflects his absolute rejection of the ugliness of domination and his insistence that love is the essential force of the universe and that it will conquer all aggression. Cardenal strips away many of our conventional thoughts about love and leaves us with a profound but simple philosophy which could be summed up as 'Love is, all else is not'.*

One thinks of St John and his long, convoluted, but beautiful

* Preface by Thomas Merton to *Love*, Ernesto Cardenal (Search Press)

discourses on love and his exhortation to love.* We are left with the simple but profound philosophy: 'God is love.' The phrase makes a very powerful mantra in prayer: reversing the words occasionally: 'Love is God.' After a while we find we leave behind us all our pre-conceived and subjective notions of love, eros, philos, agape. We find we move from love as subjective, to love as objective – reality. For Cardenal, the only reality: love is all.

In the process we come to see life, love, God, from a mystic's rather than from a moralist's point of view. Thomas Merton, in the preface to Cardenal's book, argues that moralists sometimes tell us that love is one of many virtues that are necessary to a world where there is integrity, honesty and truth. Moralists distinguish virtues from vices, and see life as the complex interaction of these. By contrast, mystics make no such distinctions; for them love is everything. Merton goes on to suggest that the only distinction mystics make is between love that is alive and well, and love that is disabled or weakened and which refuses to be what it is meant to be.

Perhaps an analogy might help us here. Scientists tell us that more than 90 per cent of all life – human, animal, plant, insect, reptile – is water. Dehydrate me and I would be no more than a little pile of dust on the floor. It is a scientific truth. I accept it. Cardenal applies the same kind of principle to all life, except that with love there would be no residue because love is all.

To use another analogy, I sometimes refer to prayer as 'Son-bathing'. That is, being still in the presence of Christ and allowing him to bathe us with the warmth and light of his love. Far from being dried up to nothing, by the Son's rays we are filled out to bursting point with the renewing and revitalising love of God. In the same way that we need vitamin D from the sun, we need to Son-bathe regularly if we are not to die of a kind of spiritual malnu-trition. Filled out by God, ultimately, there is room for nothing else.

Ordinary folk like us, who are both mystic and moralist, experi-ence conflict; we wrestle with the nature of love. We think of the summary of the Commandments, given to us by Jesus: 'You shall

* 1 John 4:7-12

love the Lord your God with all your heart, with all your mind, with all your strength. Love your neighbour as yourself.'* We try to put love into compartments – Love God, love our neighbour – as if there were two kinds of love. There is only one kind of love but there are two objects of love: God and humankind. As we learn to find God in others, the distinction becomes blessedly blurred until there is but one object of love. We were created in the image and likeness of God and we are called to love God in our neighbour who reflects the image of God himself. There is no real distinction between God and neighbour: there is only one love, and one call to love God with *all* our heart, mind, soul, strength.

Because we are human we reflect the love of God imperfectly. We look for love, for God in each other, and we glimpse it. Sometimes it shines out but mostly we see in a glass darkly, a mirror dimly – sometimes very dimly!† What we glimpse is the God who is Love.

The process is one of aiming to love like Christ loves: to love God perfectly as he loves us. We may think of this as counsel for perfection and, yes, it is, but then we are called to be perfect.‡ Mystics and moralists acknowledge that we live in a world where love and loving are far from perfect; we speak of the 'real world'. But the mystics challenge what we mean by 'real'. They argue that God is the only reality, but they show us by their lives, as well as by their words, that they understand our reality. They tell us that every love which is not totally free, spontaneous and self-giving harbours a taste of death; yet it is still a love, not yet pure or free. They want us to accept this love, fully conscious of its imperfections, so that our love may be made perfect.

This love, we know, must live in contradiction to itself. Even as there is love, there is hate. There is love and greed, love and fear, love and envy, love and lust, but it is a love destined to become love without any self-contradictory admixture.

Again Cardenal argues the point that there is only love: imperfect, yes, but in the process of being made perfect. All the less worthy attributes – what we call vices – are the names we give to imperfect

* Mark 12:29-31   † 1 Corinthians 13:12   ‡ Matthew 5:8

love. The alternative to this thinking would be that there is only Love (perfect love, God) and void, or a whole realm of created unworthiness, the fruit of another creator.

We are taught that the ultimate enemy of Love is death but Cardenal even brings death into the economy of God, thus redeeming it. He says that the basic contradiction which love has to face is the contradiction between life and death, temporal death. If death is an absurd idea, why did Christ have to die on the cross? To become Christ-like, God-like, Love-like, we must face a million little deaths. Choices must be made. The process of growing in love – for an individual, a couple, a community, a nation – is a process of dying to self so that love may reign.

We can test out this philosophy by applying it to human situations. We understand the kiss, the caress. We know, too, of possessiveness, domestic violence, abuse. We know of, or hear of, powerful forces destroying the weak and the vulnerable. Cardenal would argue that even in the ugliest and most repulsive of situations there is a love struggling for expression, but it has gone all wrong, disastrously wrong. We may know of situations where a man, who loves his wife, under certain circumstances has been known to hit her. What are we to conclude? That he does not love her or else he wouldn't do it? That there is no love at all; that he hates her, or whatever we call the void left by an absence of love; or that he loves his wife imperfectly? Which of us loves perfectly?

The moralist in us will condemn the action. The mystic in us will ask why a person's love is weakened? What is stopping it from becoming strong and from being expressed in a more Christ-like way? It may be that the man is unable to communicate his anger or frustration in a wholesome way. Enabling him to communicate effectively may bring down the barrier to more wholesome, God-like love.

Giving more attention to God, to Love, we seek to fulfil the first commandment and, in so doing our love becomes more like that of God. Our orientation having changed, our behaviour begins to change: we change. But how does love behave?

St Paul gives us that great discourse on love in his first letter to the Corinthians, Chapter 13. Consider verses 4 and 5a. 'Love is patient and kind; love is not jealous or boastful; it is not arrogant or rude. Love does not insist on its own way; it is not irritable or resentful.'

Following Cardenal's logic, there are only two kinds of people in the world and each of us is both of them. They are lovers and those who are loved. So if the lover behaves impatiently, rudely, jealously, irritably, are we to conclude that they are no lover at all? Scripture says love is patient, never rude, is not irritable. Anything which behaves like that is not love. Our intuition, our heart, tells us that cannot be true.

If St Paul had written the word 'perfect' before each of his examples, we might have understood things differently: perfect love is always patient and kind, perfect love is never jealous or boastful, perfect love is not arrogant or rude. Surely Paul was making some sort of assumption that we would understand that. Cardenal says that Love is all there is: Love, as God, behaves like this. Whatever applies to human loving must link back into the way the love of God behaves. Pure eros, pure philos, pure agape: all is love of a kind and comes from God.

Too long has the eros love of the Valentine's Day card been thought of as a less worthy love than the noble philos that binds us together as brothers and sisters. Too long has little Eros been hidden under the dark habit of St Augustine so that agape is all. But, then, I blame St Augustine for all sorts of things!

Worthy, wholesome love – whatever its name in the Greek – behaves as God behaves. Those verses from 1 Corinthians 13 are a description of God. The one verse we might struggle with is verse 4.

In the Old Testament we read, 'I the Lord thy God am a jealous God.'* If love is all there is, and love is never jealous, how does that fit in? Here we are in danger of being seduced by the limitations of our modern language since the definition of jealousy was 'zeal or solicitude'. St Paul himself qualifies this for us in his second letter to the Corinthians when he says, 'I feel a divine jealousy for you'. So love can be jealous! If we are jealous like God is jealous, we do not sin but express love the way he does, in zeal and solicitude.

* Exodus 20:5

The clue to a fresh understanding of Paul's teaching lies in 'When the perfect comes, the imperfect will pass away',* and in the image of 'passing away' we have the motif of death. For perfect love to reign, something has to go. How obvious that is. Every time we are enabled to reject the imperfect in favour of the more perfect, something passes away, a mini-death occurs. By heeding God's call to a more perfect loving, a choice has to be made, and sometimes that choice is painful. It ranges from the discomfort we feel when an apology sticks in our throat, to the complete exhaustion, stress, and humiliation we experience when we throw ourselves at the feet of someone we have hurt and take all that they can throw at us.

In Chapter Four we reflected on the basic goodness of God's creation. If we decide that we are evil creatures, where is our creator? There is only one Creator and he looked on everything he had made 'and behold, it was very good'.† Are we to hold that it is a struggle for us to do any good thing; that we are tied to a post marked 'Alienation and Annihilation' by a length of elastic. Even as we strain forward in our efforts to behave in a worthy way, we sense that, any moment, our strength will fail and we will spring back to the alienation post. At each attempt to strain forward we are further exhausted, and our head spins from hitting, again, the alienation post. Maybe we do not truly understand that there is no length of elastic, no harness. Maybe we do not understand that we are created in the image and likeness of Love, and are set free to return God's love in us; and that by so doing we can commune with God in others, and all within the life of the Trinity, rendering us never that far from the centre of Love. If we are caught in anything, it is in the mesh of interactive love between God and his creation.

Such tension as there is might be the sense of being drawn deeper into Love. We might become less imperfect, even by the tiniest degree: less likely to love imperfectly in ways that manifest themselves in hate, resentment, selfishness, greed; so that, little by little, the jealousy we exhibit becomes more like the jealousy of

* 1 Corinthians 13:10   † Genesis 1:31

God in zeal and solicitude. The pain of loss, if we are honest, is wistfulness for the sin we have had to let go in the pursuit of love.

We cannot achieve this by our own effort, only by the transforming grace of God. We come to see that it is not in our striving to do loving things, or to behave in a loving way, but the degree to which we allow love to be all in all to us. The behavioural changes follow both naturally and supernaturally. Striving to behave better is an active thing; it has more to do with lengths of elastic than anything else. Cardenal, Merton and others would urge us to focus on God, on Love as noun, and to let the transforming power of God's Spirit do the rest. Love as verb is perhaps no more than a gauge that measures how effective the transformation is becoming. To focus on love as verb at the expense of Love as noun is like breathing on a thermometer to make the mercury rise; it doesn't make the room any warmer and it exhausts us in the effort.

This contemplative, passive approach to the transforming grace of God has been expounded by the saints in every generation. The more we open ourselves to this, the more we drink deeply of God and him alone, the more we find ourselves in deeper harmony, not only with our fellow human beings – themselves repositories of God – but with the whole of Creation which is, itself, Love. 'As for prophecies, they will pass away. If there are tongues of ecstasy, they will cease.'* What abides is faith, hope, love, and the greatest of these is love: for love is God: God is love. God is the love in our lives – the life in our Loving. It is the summit of the Fruit of the Spirit and the place where we find God.

Now that we have climbed the hill of virtue, are we rendered breathless by the view, by the enormity and the beauty of virtue in the world around us, or are we left breathless by the effort of the climb? If the latter has been our experience, it may be sensible to take further journeys of discovery more gently, content with slow progress in the discovering of virtue, rejoicing where we find it, like discovering a tiny wild flower in a crevice in a wall. Perhaps we have discovered that virtue 'hill-walking' takes effort and a little discipline. The passivity of contemplation can so easily mask the effort that

* 1 Corinthians 13:8

goes into it. Whether accompanied by others along the way, or walking quietly alone, I hope the journey has been worthwhile and the discovery, or rediscovery, of the God of virtue, revealed in his people, a blessing.

Focus for reflection

God is love, and those who abide in love, abide in God.
1 John 4:16b

Questions for discussion

1. Do you distinguish between different kinds of love?
2. Is imperfect love genuine love?
3. St Paul says love hopes all things, believes all things, endures all things. In what ways does this compare with your experience of love?

Group activity

• Having completed the summit of your garden of virtue and lit all nine candles, you may like to compose a tune to the words of St Paul in Galatians 5:22-23 and sing it together in celebration.

• Alternatively, you may want to sing a hymn or song that expresses all that you have come to appreciate about the God who makes himself present in virtue.

Suggestions for prayer

Lord,
you love us with a perfect love.
There are no constraints on your love:
it is boundless!
How hard it is, Lord, to make sense of that
when we know how imperfectly we love you!
Help us to celebrate your loving presence in all your creation,
wherever we discover it,
and no matter how well it is disguised.
Amen.

God's Good Fruit

Accept, Lord, my poor offering of love
and wrap me in your loving embrace,
so that something more of your love
might be squeezed into me.
Amen.

Lord,
where would I be without the love I have received
from you and from others.
From before my birth your love has sustained me, healed me,
and made it possible for me to love in return (even imperfectly).
Amen.